The Agony & Glory *of the* Cross

The Agony & Glory of the Cross

Charles B. Hodge, Jr.

RESOURCE □
PUBLICATIONS
2205 S. Benton
Searcy, AR 72143

ISBN-13: 978-0-9760327-7-9
ISBN-10: 0-9760327-7-5

Contents

Preface

All Christians and all preachers have only one message . . . the cross. Paul said, "For I determined to know nothing among you except Jesus Christ, and Him crucified" (1 Corinthians 2:2). We love the Word and use the Word, yet we do not study the Word or live the Word. While we wear the cross as jewelry and use it on our signs, it was meant to be only for the heart. In 1980 I determined to preach on the cross in all my revivals. Two years later I wrote an entire series of lessons on this topic. In 1985 every sermon in my local work focused upon Christ.

The cross mandates death. It is gory, bloody, and demanding. While writing is difficult, writing on the cross is more difficult. To touch the cross is to defile it. No one can do justice to it. You preach, teach, and write—then cry because you did not do better. This study now for years has been a wrestling match. It is holy ground. It has been humbling, overwhelming, yet rewarding. Did you notice what Paul said in his statement? The cross is not superficial—it is the depth of *all* knowledge! Christians must come to "know" the Christ, the cross! This is our glory.

As you study these lessons, allow the cross to speak for itself.

*"God forbid that I should glory,
save in the cross of our Lord Jesus Christ"
(Galatians 6:14a; KJV).*

Charles B. Hodge, Jr.

1

"Li'l Abner" was a popular 1930s comic strip by Al Capp. Among its special characters and situations, one of the often used quotations was "It is more confusing than amusing." This phrase is used in this series to introduce some ideas that are meant to be thought-provoking as one studies the cross. In each chapter, the "More Confusing than Amusing" section allows for special meditation before the study of the lesson.

"MORE CONFUSING THAN AMUSING"

THE OFFENSE OF THE CROSS

"God forbid that I should glory, save in the cross of our Lord Jesus Christ" (Galatians 6:14a; KJV). You cannot have the glory of the cross without the agony of the cross. The heart of God is revealed at the cross. Satan tries to remove the cross from Christ and His church. To understand the "offense," therefore, is crucial. God and culture are always at "cross" purposes. If you do not understand the "offense," then you have missed the gospel! To miss here is to miss completely! God said it all at the cross. What more could He say? The cross is too important to be left to theologians.

Sermons, the church, songs, books, art, and daily conversations all vibrate with the cross. How, then, can there be any offense in it? They talk of "sweet baby Jesus," "a helpless man dying on a cross!" They view Him as "harmless." They view the story of the cross as a sentimental fairy tale. Popular preaching has removed the violence, blood, and cruelty inherent in the cross; it has made the cross painless and sterile.

No one today has seen a crucifixion. It was humiliating beyond words. No one can grasp the agony of the cross. We design our church architecture using the cross but do not count the cost of living for Christ. The cross is not an idol; it is not "a religious story." Men glorify the cross rather than the Christ on the cross. The cross is not sentimental nonsense; it is historic and real.

We love life; the cross is death. We want victory; the cross is defeat. We want peace; the cross is war. We love beauty; the cross is ugly. The cross is diametrically different from the desires of mankind. Critics protest, "How dare God be God!" Nevertheless, He is!

Jesus sternly told His disciples that He would offend people (Matthew 16:16–23; 26:31–35; Mark 8:27–33; John 6:60, 61). Christ even used a word meaning "scandalized,"[1] saying His followers would be offended (Mark 14:27–31). It is very difficult today for believers to see the offense of the cross. It was difficult then.

Who could accept a crucified common criminal as Savior? In polite Roman society, the word "cross" was an obscenity and was not to be used. This was too much for Peter; he tried to protect Jesus. He was agitated. Jesus reacted quickly to Peter, identifying him with Satan! (Matthew 16:23). We do not like Jesus acting like Jesus! However, this was the battleground for Jesus. He "sweated blood" in Gethsemane, trying to avoid the cross (Luke 22:40–44). People can manage their enemies, but they cannot manage their friends. Jesus had to react quickly and firmly. Peter also knew Scripture. The tree (cross) was a curse (Deuteronomy 21:23; Acts 5:30; Galatians 3:13).

---

[1]The Greek word for "scandalized," *skandalizo,* means to fall away.

Paul was not ashamed of the gospel (Romans 1:16, 17). Are we? The temptation is always to remove, to minimize the cross. Paul talked about "the offense of the cross" in Galatians 5:11 (NKJV). He also revealed Christ as "a rock of offense" (Romans 9:31–33). He taught the cross as a stumbling block for the Jews and foolishness to the Gentiles (1 Corinthians 1:17–25).

God's "punctuation mark" in history is in the shape of the cross. You do not understand Jesus until you understand the cross. At the cross God said it was better to bring good out of evil than not to allow evil at all. If the cross does not matter, then nothing matters!

Nothing on earth is as controversial, offensive, or divisive as the cross. No one ever made people angrier than Jesus did!

The cross offends because God, not man, is right. (1) God is right because our problem is *sin*. (2) God is right because the only answer to *sin* is the *cross*! Sinners are lost, damned, and hell-bound. This offends us. Man cannot admit that he is lost enough to need salvation. Sinners do not wish to know, or to be reminded, of their guilt. Preachers are constantly reminded not to declare that sinners are "sinners." This contradicts our proud, selfish, stubborn, and sinful hearts. Christ died for the ungodly, for sinners (Romans 5:6–8). I qualify!

The cross offends because sinners do not deserve, cannot earn, and cannot buy salvation. We see here the offense of grace! Jesus paid it all. Grace is not a license to sin; it does not rid sinners of responsibility. What justice demanded, grace provided. Jesus is the "Lamb of God" (John 1:29, 36). He was not only rejected by man (John 1:10, 11), but He was also forsaken by God (Matthew 27:46). Sinful man is eternally helpless without Jesus! Without the cross, there can be no crown. Man cannot imagine or explain the cross—he can only humbly believe. This offends.

Jesus said, "I am the way, and the truth, and the life; no one comes to the Father but through Me" (John 14:6). This is rigid, narrow, exclusive, intolerant, and judgmental . . . but it is the truth. Such is offensive (see Acts 4:11, 12). Do we seek to please men or God? (John 12:42, 43; Acts 5:29). No sinner can be saved apart from Jesus. The time has come to put the cross back into Christianity. "'And I, if I am lifted up from the earth, will draw all men to Myself.' But He was saying this to indicate the kind of death by which He was to die" (John 12:32, 33). God Himself . . . gave Himself . . . to save us . . . from Himself!

The Week That Changed The World

Matthew 21—27; Mark 11—15; Luke 19:29—23:53; John 11:55—19:42

"After they had mocked Him, they took the scarlet robe off Him and put His own garments back on Him, and led Him away to crucify Him" (Matthew 27:31).

This was the week of weeks! The week when God (Jesus) died! The week of God's greatest work (the cross)! It is overwhelming! This is our highest privilege: God's greatest treasure is preached by earthen vessels (2 Corinthians 4:7).

The Gospels reveal only forty-plus days in the life of Christ, yet the narration of this week goes into detail concerning His activities. One-third of the Gospels center upon this week; it makes up one-half of the Gospel of John. They are telling us that this week is crucial. During His ministry Jesus avoided Jerusalem. Now, He set His face toward Jerusalem (Luke 9:51). Jesus was in total control; He went to Jerusalem to die.

What did Jesus do? He taught and taught! He was teaching even on the cross! The church is here to teach, teach, teach! Never has the church taught less! In 1985 I gave all of my local sermons on Christ. That was my most criticized year in preaching! The Jews claimed to want the Messiah, yet when He came they had Him crucified! He did not fulfill their concept of a Messiah. Does He fit ours? Can we accept the biblical Christ? Jesus was teaching until the bitter end.

Let us look at the week that changed the world. All eternity comes down to this week.

SUNDAY . . .
A DAY OF ACCLAIM

The Anointing
(Matthew 26:6–13; Mark 14:3–9;
John 12:1–8)

On Sunday, the first event was the anointing of Jesus.[2] He was at Bethany in the house of Simon the leper: "So they made Him a supper there, and Martha was serving; but Lazarus was one of those reclining at the table with Him" (John 12:2). After an admonition to Martha during another visit, Jesus still ate what Martha had cooked (Luke 10:38–42).

Throughout His life Jesus had given, not received. That changed on this day. Perhaps it is easier to give than to receive. Jesus taught both. Mary anointed Jesus with expensive oil. Its worth was approximately a year's wages for a common man.

The true character of Judas surfaces here as he said,

---

[2]Remember that while our day begins and ends at midnight, the Jewish day began at 6:00 p.m. Therefore, the supper at Simon's house was on Sunday. John gave chronological clues regarding the dinner and the anointing: Jesus arrived in Bethany six days before the Passover (John 12:1), and then the Triumphal Entry took place "on the next day" after the meal (John 12:12).

"Why was this perfume not sold for three hundred denarii and given to poor people? . . ." (John 12:4–6). It is amazing how the apostles could openly criticize and condemn Jesus! Their rebuke of Jesus was harsh, not nice.

True friends are costly. Jesus had resurrected His friend Lazarus (John 11). That resurrection played a part in crucifying Jesus. Our good works can cause hate and persecution.

Benevolence is a blessing to us and to others. Serving Jesus is of even greater importance. Whatever is given to Jesus for Jesus cannot be titled "waste." Jesus exposed Judas' guilty motives, and He honored Mary's extravagance of love. Anything love gives is always too little.

The Triumphal Entry
(Matthew 21:1–11; Mark 11:1–11;
Luke 19:29–41; John 12:12–15)

Jesus had never had a "party." Since men would not do it, He gave Himself one. He forced people to make a decision: "Accept Me or kill Me!" He was ready for attack; He totally orchestrated "The Triumphal Entry."

He sent two disciples to get a colt that had never been ridden. This is amazing! Farmers would rarely allow this. Then people spread branches and their clothes upon the road. Jesus had a parade! The people shouted, "Hosanna," which means "Save, we pray." This entrance fulfilled Zechariah 9:9.

As Jesus arrived at Jerusalem, He was overcome with emotion—His heart was broken. He cried over Jerusalem (Luke 19:41). Before we preach to the world, we need to cry over it.

Jesus rode into town peacefully. The Romans were

not bothered. How fickle man is! The crowd on Sunday were Galileans, but the crowd on Thursday and Friday were Judeans. The Prince of Peace came to town honored by the "Hallel Psalms."[3] However, this forced the Pharisees to take action. They thought the world had gone after Him (John 12:19). Parades are as much for those who watch as for those who are honored.

The Pharisees were horrified! They commanded Jesus to rebuke (or silence) the disciples, but Jesus refused. If His disciples had not praised Him, the stones would have cried out (Luke 19:40).

Jesus had His parade. What will we do with it?

MONDAY . . .
A DAY OF AUTHORITY

Jesus had now arrived in Jerusalem. He could never be "Man of the Year" on the cover of a magazine or receive the Nobel Peace Prize, but He is our Savior! He rode on a donkey (a symbol of peace); He did not ride on a horse (a symbol of war). Since Solomon, no king had ridden on a donkey.

The donkey He rode was not even His; it was borrowed. Jesus was a "Pauper King." He went to the subjects; usually subjects go to their king.

Jesus cried over Jerusalem. It had been God's chosen city. Ten thousand memories were vanishing; time was running out. Jerusalem was about to be totally destroyed (A.D. 67–70).

The parade was monumental, but we must see be-

---

[3]"Hallel" means "praise." The Hallel Psalms (113—115) were sung throughout the year but were used in their entirety during Jewish feasts, including the Passover. (Compare Matthew 21:9 and Psalm 118:26.)

yond the parade. While Jerusalem had refuse(
the people could not refuse to *see*! The issue, as aₗᵥₐ, .
was authority. Jesus presented His credentials.

Jesus Cursed a Fig Tree
(Matthew 21:18–22; Mark 11:12–14, 20–26)

Jesus was hungry. He saw a fig tree with leaves and was disappointed to find no fruit. He damned this tree forever. This is not nice, and this is not the Jesus most of us have created in our minds. This action is one of only two negative (destructive) miracles of Jesus (see Matthew 8:28–34). It harmed nature, but not humanity. He was giving an object lesson that the apostles had to learn. The sin is pride; the sin is hypocrisy. The fig tree claimed to have fruit. It did not. Jewish leaders claimed to be of God. They were not. The Jews should have been humbled to be called by God. Instead, they thought they were superior, invincible.

Peter was amazed by the sudden death of that fig tree. We should be amazed with Peter and the other apostles. They had seen Jesus walk on water, heal the sick, and raise the dead. Still, they were shocked to see the fig tree wither! How blind can we be?

Jesus Cleansed the Temple
(Matthew 21:12–15; Mark 11:15–19; Luke 19:45–48)

Jesus went straight to the temple. Without introduction, He began teaching. On the side He healed the blind and the lame. The chief priests and the scribes saw the marvelous things He did (Matthew 21:15). The temple area was to be reverenced. How it was abused! The people were using it as a shortcut through Jerusalem.

As He cleansed the temple, Jesus did not attack men,

but He did run them out. He did rearrange the furniture. He quoted the Bible: "'My house shall be called a house of prayer'; but you are making it a robbers' den" (Matthew 21:13; see Jeremiah 7:11). He was not a coward or a "sissy." He was a "man among men." He not only was physically strong, but also used the Scriptures mightily. His language was harsh but true.

Jesus Continued His Teaching
(John 12:20–50)

In the midst of all this, a delegation of Greeks came, wanting to see Jesus (John 12:20). While the Jews sought to kill Him, the Greeks sought to hear Him! Philip was always bringing someone to Jesus. Partnered with Andrew, he approached Jesus. Jesus knew "His hour" had come, yet He continued to teach profound truths. He taught that seed must die to live and that those who love their lives lose them (John 12:21–26). Then Jesus added, "Father, glorify Your name." For a third time in the life of Christ, heaven spoke (John 12:28). To some it sounded like thunder, but to Jesus it was a promise of victory. Satan was to be cast out. Jesus declared, "And I, if I am lifted up from the earth, will draw all men to Myself" (John 12:32).

This truth was taught to Jews, not Greeks. In spite of this glorious teaching with miracles, the Pharisees refused to believe. Jesus concluded, ". . . they loved the approval of men rather than the approval of God" (John 12:42, 43).

TUESDAY . . .
A DAY OF ACTIVITY

Of the days recorded in the Scriptures, Tuesday was the busiest day in the life of Christ. When Jesus cleansed the temple, He hit the Jewish leaders in their pocketbooks. This got their attention. The Jews had to pay the temple tax with the Hebrew shekel. Those coming to Jerusalem had to exchange their Roman denarii or Greek drachmas into shekels in order to pay the tax. The money changers charged an exorbitant amount. They were a "robbers' den" even at "church."

They became angry with Jesus and asked, "Where did you get your authority?"; "Who are you?"; "Who do you think you are?" They thought they could quickly run this Galilean out of town. If He answered, "God," He lost; if He answered, "Man," He still lost. However, Jesus turned the situation around by asking, "Where did John the Baptist get his authority?" Jesus fought fire with fire. They refused to answer. So did He! (Matthew 21:23–27; Mark 11:27–33; Luke 20:1–8). The Jewish leaders tried to demean Jesus: "What are your credentials? You are not a priest, an ordained rabbi, a graduate of Jerusalem Seminary." In spite of this, He was "the Great Debater." He exposed their foolishness.

Jesus taught three parables in this context. The apostles asked Jesus why He did this and what He meant (Matthew 13:10, 36). This practice eliminated from His followers those who were merely curious. Parables are not "children's stories." Parables gently guide you to convict yourself. Urgently, Jesus preached with all His heart. He presented the parable of the two sons (Matthew 21:28–32). Publicans and harlots will enter into God's presence when some "church folk" will not. Publicans and harlots did not crucify Jesus. It was done by God's nation, Israel. This was God's town, Jerusalem. In it was God's temple, but in it Jesus would soon be crucified. It is shocking to see how vicious, blind, proud, and prejudiced religionists can be.

Next, Jesus told the parable of the wicked renters who killed the landlord's son (Matthew 21:33–41; Mark 12:1–12; Luke 20:9–19). He spoke of the stone that could have saved Israel but was cast aside. The leaders knew that Jesus was talking straight to them. He told the parable of the marriage feast (Matthew 22:2–14). Relatives and friends not only rejected the invitation, but they even used the occasion for murderous sport. The king who was having the wedding for his son was furious and said, "Go therefore to the main highways, and as many as you find there, invite to the wedding feast" (Matthew 22:9). When the privileged shut themselves out, the common were invited. No wonder the common people heard Jesus gladly (Mark 12:37).

Then the Pharisees and the Herodians allied to entangle Jesus in His words. The Pharisees hated the Herodians and believed they were traitors—but they hated Jesus more. The next trick question was presented: "What about the poll tax?" Jesus, holding a coin, said, "Render to Caesar the things that are Caesar's; and to God the things that are God's" (Matthew 22:21). This shocked them into silence. Then the Sadducees offered silliness. Jesus was not even gentle with them. He said, "You don't know the Scriptures"; "You don't know the power of God" (Matthew 22:29–34). The persistent Pharisees returned with a lawyer, who asked, "What is the great command?" Jesus answered, "Love God foremost," and then added the second greatest: "Love your neighbor." Next, Jesus asked them who the Messiah really was. They offered no response; the debates ended.

Following all of this, He preached the most scathing sermon in the Scriptures (Matthew 23). We know it is in the Bible, but we usually do not connect it with the cross. He called Jewish leaders "snakes," "blind guides," and "hypocrites." He pronounced seven woes, in which He branded them "fools." "How can you escape the condemnation of hell?" He asked. Then He cried, "O Jerusalem, Jerusalem" (Matthew 23:37; Luke 13:34).

As they walked away from the temple, the disciples asked Jesus questions: "When will these things be?"; "What will be the sign of Your coming?"; "When is the end of the age?" Jesus dealt with these questions in Matthew 24, Mark 13, and Luke 21. He was still teaching, teaching, teaching. In this context comes the "widow with the two mites" (Mark 12:41–44). Amidst all the hypocrisy, God sent this humble widow to remind His Son who He was and what He had come to do. What a God!

Trouble! In spite of the crowds and the critics, Jesus taught His disciples three profound parables: the parable of the ten virgins, the parable of the talents, and the parable of the sheep and the goats (Matthew 25:1–30). No man ever preached as Jesus did that day, but His preaching fell on deaf ears.

What a day!

WEDNESDAY . . .
A DAY OF NO ACTIVITY

After the argumentative wars on Tuesday, God gave Jesus a day off. He vanished. We do not know where He was, with whom He spent that day, or what He did. The silence thunders! The Pharisees had rejoiced over the rout of the Sadducees by Jesus, but their humor quickly turned to hatred when Jesus silenced them. Jesus was "The Great Debater." His enemies reasoned, "Since we cannot answer Him, we must kill Him."

Jesus may not have been busy on this day, but Judas was. His betrayal was not impulsive—it was deliberate. The Sanhedrin was also busy—it met in a secret session. Satan, too, was busy. He did succeed in killing Jesus, but that "victory" was his eternal defeat. Wednesday was the calm before the storm. Wouldn't you say that Jesus spent that day with God?

THURSDAY . . .
A DAY OF ACTION

Jesus awoke Thursday never to sleep again. The "hour" had come. Following a respite on Wednesday, Jesus renewed His march to the cross. He was in total control. Others thought they were, but they were not. Jesus initiated and forced the cross. He was determined but not in a hurry.

The objective for this day was to prepare the Passover meal (Matthew 26:17–19; Mark 14:12–16; Luke 22:7–13). Jesus told His disciples to find and follow a man carrying a pitcher of water. This is fascinating! He would be the only man in Jerusalem doing that, for it was "women's work." The apostles did as Jesus said. A room was found prepared. Consider how amazing this is! They needed a large room. The Passover was for a group. Jerusalem was overflowing with people. There could be no empty rooms. Not only was this room empty, but it was also ready! How could this be? God's awesome providence! God is at work in our lives. He can make impossible things possible.

Jesus had a fervent interest in eating this Passover with the apostles (Luke 22:14–16). Several reasons can be given: (1) Jesus announced this in reference to His suffering. He wanted and needed their companionship.

(2) This was to be God's last Passover meal. Jesus nailed the law of Moses to the cross (Colossians 2:14). What God gave, God took away. (3) Jesus is now our continuous Passover (1 Corinthians 5:7). (4) In this situation Jesus initiated His Supper.

Two things command our attention: the authority of the Scriptures and Jesus' obedience. Jesus kept God's law! He was born, lived, and died under the Law. He obeyed the Law to the letter and in the right spirit (Matthew 5:17–20). *Do not devalue the Scriptures. Oppose false teachers and false teaching.*

We now come to Thursday night, the Jewish Friday. As Jesus was about to die, the apostles fussed over who was the greatest (Luke 22:24–30; see John 13:1–20). Could it be that Judas was involved in this? He had led in the tirade against Mary and the anointing (John 12:1–8). He was rebuffed for that.

Every group has to have a leader or leaders. Someone must be responsible. Jesus designated Peter, James, and John. Could there have been resentment, jealousy, or a power struggle? Judas, as treasurer, perhaps had some influence. Obviously, he was affected by power and control.

Judas' betrayal of Jesus was no impulsive decision. The seating at the meal could have triggered the outburst, but the problem was far greater. Jesus had taught against the heathen idolatry of power, saying, "It is not this way among you" (Matthew 20:20–28; see Luke 22:24–27). James and John (with their mother) had requested special privilege and power. Jesus said much about "pushing and shoving" for chief seats (see Matthew 23:6–12; Mark 12:38–40). Their problem is our problem.

How did Jesus handle this? He did not yell, threaten,

or harshly rebuke. If I had been Jesus, I would have prayed to God, "I need a whole new group of disciples!" Instead, quietly, He taught and taught! He picked up a towel and washed their feet (see John 13:1–15). The silence was deafening. It was shattered by Peter's outburst: "You will never wash my feet." Firmly, yet gently, Jesus silenced Peter. The Son of God built His church with a towel. He declared Himself to be "The Servant" (see Luke 22:27). He then began the first of many warnings to His apostles, but they were without success. It is easier to wash feet than to be washed. Jesus washed the feet of those who were present and would have also washed Judas' feet. Could this act have pushed Judas across the line?

At the Passover meal, Jesus announced the betrayal that was coming. Because of what we now know, we might think of Judas as being the unanimous choice to be the betrayer, but that was not the case. The apostles did not believe that another one among them would betray the Lord . . . but each thought he could (Matthew 26:21–25; Mark 14:18–21; Luke 22:21–23; John 13:21–30). Judas asked, "Is it I?" (Matthew 26:25; John 13:26, 27; NKJV). Jesus gave him the sop. Amazingly, the other apostles totally missed it. Judas knew that Jesus knew! Years ago, Reuel Lemmons had a provocative sermon entitled, "And It Was Night," based on John 13:30, which says, "So after receiving the morsel [Judas] went out immediately; and it was night." God is light; sin is darkness. Judas left the light for the darkness. Satan's entrance into Judas was not mystical or supernatural. Judas allowed and welcomed him in. *Do not leave light for darkness.*

After Jesus dismissed Judas, He instituted His Supper

. . . the Lord's Supper (Matthew 26:26–29; Mark 14:22–25; Luke 22:17–20; 1 Corinthians 10:16–21; 11:23–30). John 6:48–60 is not a reference to the Lord's Supper, but it is doctrinal truth. To be saved we must ingest Christ—His life, doctrine, and salvation. The Lord's Supper was initiated in an assembly. The early church assembled to partake (Acts 20:7; 1 Corinthians 10; 11). New Testament worship glories in its simplicity—bread and a cup. En route to His death, Jesus was teaching, teaching, teaching. John 14 was given in the "upper room." John 15 and 16 came as Jesus moved toward Gethsemane. Judas left before Jesus gave John 13:34, 35: "A new commandment I give to you, that you love one another, even as I have loved you, that you also love one another. By this all men will know that you are My disciples, if you have love for one another." Sin does catastrophic harm; part of the tragedy is in what you miss. Judas missed so much! He never saw the risen Lord.

Jesus' attention next centered upon Peter, who vowed unlimited allegiance. He stated that before the rooster crowed, Peter would deny Him three times (Matthew 26:33–35; John 13:36–38). Luke offers more detail (22:31–34). Satan desired Peter, but Jesus said He had prayed for him. Had Jesus equally prayed for Judas?

FRIDAY . . .
A DAY OF AGONY

It was a long night. Jesus crossed the Brook Kidron and headed to Gethsemane. Little is known about where, when, and how Jesus prayed "The High Priestly Prayer," the real "Lord's Prayer" (John 17). This prayer is perhaps the greatest prayer ever prayed! He prayed for His apostles, Himself, and us!

Gethsemane! This prayer is the most difficult one ever prayed. The entire human race was at stake. Jesus' decision was made in Gethsemane—not at Golgotha. This is where God said no and Jesus said yes (Matthew 26:36–46; Mark 14:32–42; Luke 22:40–46). There was more pain in Gethsemane than on Calvary. The "sweat like blood" fell in Gethsemane (Luke 22:44). Jesus was in an agony "to the point of death" in this garden. No man ever suffered as Jesus suffered then. The greatest battle He fought was in prayer. This was the "Holy of Holies" in the life of Christ. His final teaching ended in prayer.

Jesus left eight of the apostles, taking Peter, James, and John deeper into the garden. He left these three with the command to "keep watching and praying" (Matthew 26:41). He fell on His face, His nose in the dirt, to pray the same prayer three times: ". . . let this cup pass from Me" (Matthew 26:39; Mark 14:36; Luke 22:42). Critics pounce upon this prayer, suggesting a lack of courage, perhaps cowardice. That is blasphemy! It would contradict everything Jesus *is*! He had come too far to give up now. Jesus was not a coward. He was not afraid of death, pain, or the cross. He was not asking God to abort the cross and substitute another way. This cross was God's eternal purpose. He was not performing drama, mysticism, magic, or novelty. He was in an agony unto death. His sweat *did* drop like blood.

What was this "cup"? The battle of all eternity was to be fought between God and Satan. The winner would take all. Humanity was at stake. Jesus fought to conquer Satan, sin, death, and hell . . . alone! On the cross He cried, "My God, My God, why have You forsaken Me?" (Matthew 27:46; Mark 15:34). (1) He was made to be what God hated—sin. (2) The eternal wrath of a holy God was poured out upon Him. (3) This was the only time in all eternity that God the Father and Christ the Son were separated. Horror of horrors! Jesus did not want out of this arrangement to save mankind. He was never arrogant in His humanity. God answered Jesus' prayer immediately. An angel came to strengthen Him (Luke 22:43). One angel? *One?* God sent two angels to Mary Magdalene and to the women at the empty tomb (Luke 24:1–7). Jesus could have called for twelve legions of angels (Matthew 26:53). He got *one?* A supernatural miracle could not substitute for human responsibility. No man knew better than Jesus that ". . . the spirit is willing, but the flesh is weak" (Matthew 26:41; Mark 14:38). Only in humanity could sinful man be saved. The cross is of no benefit to fallen angels. Jesus went where no man could go; He, as man, did what no man could do: "In the days of His flesh, He offered up both prayers and supplications with loud crying and tears to the One able to save Him from death, and He was heard because of His piety" (Hebrews 5:7).

Even the cross did not have the anxiety of Gethsemane. The only time in Scripture Jesus called God "Abba" (Aramaic for something similar to "Daddy") was here (Mark 14:36). In Gethsemane Jesus did not hide, run, or even fight . . . He prayed. In athletics the game is won through preparation . . . decision . . . commitment. Jesus won the battle in Gethsemane. *Make the big decision before Satan shows up.*

The mob led by Judas arrived. Men in a mob lose their individuality. Hatred rejects thought. The armed mob was scared—scared to death of Jesus. They did not deny or doubt that Jesus had raised Lazarus from the dead. In fact, they considered killing him too (John 12:10). Judas was their solution; he gave them an opportunity to do the job (Mark 14:10, 11; Luke 22:3–5). Judas knew where Jesus would be and what He would be doing (praying), but he did not know Jesus. However, Judas still called Jesus "Rabbi" (Matthew 26:49). He still called him "friend" (Matthew 26:50). Was this sarcasm? Probably not. Did this aid in Judas' feeling remorse? Probably. John MacArthur said that Judas "had the behavior of a saint but the heart of a sinner."[4]

Peter, frightened, resorted to force. Can you change an idea with a club? When Jesus took Peter's sword from him, he collapsed like a tent. He warmed himself by the "devil's fire" (see Mark 14:54; John 18:18, 25). In doing this, Peter placed himself closer to the enemy than to Christ. Guard against doing this! *Always guard where you are and with whom you are spending your time.* In quick succession, Peter denied Jesus three times. Then the rooster crowed. Judas betrayed, Peter denied, the apostles scattered, Satan exulted, and the rooster crowed. Jesus then was shuttled from Annas to Caiaphas, to the Sanhedrin, to Pilate, to Herod, and back to Pilate. Peter cried (Matthew 26:75).

We must examine the plight of Judas to keep us from his sin (Matthew 27:3–10). He returned the money (thirty pieces of silver); it was worthless to him. The betrayer had remorse that comes from pride, but he did not have repentance that comes from humility. He committed suicide.

---

[4]John MacArthur, "Unmasking the Betrayer," in the "Table Talks with Jesus" series, The John MacArthur Collection, ©1983 by John F. MacArthur, Jr. (http://www.biblebb.com/mac-h-z.htm; Internet; accessed 17 November 2006).

Jewish rulers could crucify the Son of God, but they would not touch "blood money." Judas could see his mistake, but he could not see his Savior. No one despises a traitor like those who have used him.

Judas hanged himself. No one even cut him down (Acts 1:15–26). Sin has terrible consequences. The traitor "turned aside to go to his own place" (Acts 1:25) and is never mentioned again in the Scriptures. He should never have been born!

Jesus was on the cross for *six hours* before He died—from 9 a.m. until 3 p.m. Chapters 3 and 4 are devoted to these six hours. He did not have a "pre-planned funeral." Neither His family nor His apostles buried Him. Let us marvel at God's providence! He died as a pauper, but He was buried as a king! Joseph of Arimathea and Nicodemus, aided by the women, wrapped Jesus' body with linen and expensive spices and buried Him in a new tomb (Matthew 27:57–61; Mark 15:42–47; Luke 23:50–56; John 19:38–42). God takes care of His own! What happened to Joseph and Nicodemus? No one knows, yet we thank them! Some will do more for a lost cause than a living hope. It is easier to bury the dead than to obey the living Lord.

You only bury those who are dead. Pilate, Joseph, Nicodemus, and the women knew that Jesus was dead. The simplest, most certified fact about Jesus is His death.

SATURDAY . . .
A DAY OF ABSENCE

If Satan ever had a banquet in hell, it was on this Passover Sabbath when Jesus was a corpse. Jesus' resurrection is the death-knell to Sabbatarianism.

SUNDAY . . .
A DAY OF APPEARANCES

On Sunday the tomb was empty. An angel asked, "Why do you seek the living among the dead? He is not here, but is risen!" (Luke 24:5, 6a; NKJV). If there had been no empty tomb, the world would never have heard of Jesus. He appeared first to Mary Magdalene, a woman (Mark 16:1–9; John 20:1–18). Then He appeared to the other women (Matthew 28:1–8; Luke 24:1–11) and to the men on the Emmaus Road (Luke 24:13–33). He appeared to Peter (Luke 24:34) and to the eleven (Thomas was absent) (John 20:19–25). This was the week that changed the world! This was the week that also changed me!

The cross . . .
there is no other way!

QUESTIONS FOR STUDY AND DISCUSSION

1. Why is it that "if the cross does not matter, then nothing matters"?

2. Why is it important that we understand the "offense" of the cross? How does the cross offend?

3. Give reasons why the Gospels place so much emphasis upon the final week of Jesus' life.

4. How did the Triumphal Entry promote Jesus' plan?

5. Why would some people today have trouble accepting the cleansing of the temple? Why is this event significant?

6. Discuss the debates that Jesus had with the religious leaders.

7. What parables did Jesus teach on Tuesday of His final week? What was the meaning of these parables?

8. Why was this Passover feast so important to Jesus? What was on His mind? What was on the apostles' minds?

9. Judas left the light for the darkness—he was overcome with darkness. Discuss light and darkness in your spiritual life.

10. What does Gethsemane teach us about being committed to God?

11. Comment on the brevity of details concerning the crucifixion.

12. What does the resurrection mean to us?

2

"MORE CONFUSING THAN AMUSING"

GETHSEMANE

"God forbid that I should glory, save in the cross of our Lord Jesus Christ." Gethsemane! Poignant, precious, profound, and priceless!

"Gethsemane" simply means "oil press." This garden, across the brook from Jerusalem on Mt. Olivet, was Jesus' "prayer closet" when He was in Jerusalem (John 18:1, 2). Judas knew where Jesus would be in order to betray Him. He knew that Jesus would be praying—but he did not know Jesus!

We know about Jesus, but do we really know Jesus? How could Judas not know Jesus? How can we not know Jesus? Among the disciples, Jesus had a Judas. Can there be a "Judas" lurking in all of us? We must read Matthew 26, Mark 14, Luke 22, and John 18 more closely. Jesus tersely said that it would have been better if Judas had not been born (Matthew 26:24).

Prayer time! Jesus fully knew His "hour" had come. His word for this time was "cup." The weight of every sin was upon His back. He instituted the Lord's Supper. He prophesied His imminent betrayal. How disappointed, hurt, and rejected He was! Judas would betray Him; Peter would deny Him. Only one of the twelve (John) would even be at the cross. Israel would reject Him in favor of a common criminal (Barabbas). Jerusalem would gladly crucify Him! To make matters worse, His disciples were busy debating which of them was the greatest. Led by Peter, all the disciples vowed to be dependable. All failed. Jesus told Peter he would deny Him three times before the crowing of a rooster.

It was time to pray! The most dominant ministry of Christ was prayer. He had prayed before, during, and after great events. If Jesus needed prayer, how much more do we? He knelt and then fell face down. There is no contradiction here. He invited Peter, James, and John to watch with Him. They slept.

Prayer is not a guarantee that God will grant every wish. Prayer is under the will of God. Jesus reminded the Father that He was the God of the impossible! Under severe duress, the "sweat became like drops of blood" (Luke 22:44). Have you ever prayed like that? He prayed this way not just once, but three times! He prayed, "May this cup pass." His critics were right: "He saved others; He cannot save Himself" (Matthew 27:42; Mark 15:31; see Luke 23:35). God did answer Jesus' prayer! He did not spare Jesus, but He did save us! Jesus could not save Himself and still be our Savior. Jesus prayed in mental anguish with a broken heart. Still, God said no. *There is no way but the cross!*

Decision time! The battle of all time and eternity was fought in Gethsemane . . . in prayer. Eternal decisions can only be made in prayer. Nothing can be settled until prayer settles it. God (the Father) said no three times; God (the Son) said yes once. Jesus accepted the divine judgment and punishment that sin deserves. Jesus had to wrestle to yield His heart to the sacrifice demanded by God. "It is finished" was said on the cross, but it was decided in Gethsemane. Jesus gave His soul in Gethsemane; He gave His body at Golgotha.

Pain time! The Scriptures say more about suffering in Gethsemane than on the cross. In joy Jesus endured the cross (Hebrews 12:1, 2). God hates sin; Jesus was made to be what God hates. A holy God cannot touch sin. As sin, Jesus could not be touched by God. This was the only time in all eternity when God the Father abandoned God the Son (Matthew 27:46). This was the "cup" which could not be passed!

This God-forsaken Son is the centerpiece of the Christian faith. Do not minimize the physical pain of the cross. It was horrific! However, the writers of the Gospels placed little or no emphasis upon the physical. Jesus did not "sweat blood" on the cross. He did in Gethsemane (Luke 22:44). God sent an angel to Gethsemane (Luke 22:43). None were sent to Calvary. *Two* were sent to Mary at the empty tomb (John 20:11, 12).

Betrayal time! Veiled humor can be found here. Hundreds came heavily armed to arrest one unarmed preacher. Jesus stood out in the open, saying, "Here I am." The mob fell back upon the ground! The battle was won in Gethsemane before the mob arrived. Make the decision before the trial.

It was a long, hard, cold night!

The Trials

Matthew 26:57–68; 27:1, 2, 11–25;
Mark 14:53–65; 15:1–15; Luke 22:63—23:25;
John 18:2—19:16

"For many were giving false testimony against Him, but their testimony was not consistent" (Mark 14:56).

The trials were unfair from beginning to end! Jesus was treated so grossly that Satan must have blushed! Not even Satan can control sin! This has to be the lowest point in all history. Judas betrayed, Peter denied, ten apostles scattered, four puppet rulers—Annas, Caiaphas, Pilate, and Herod—judged the "Judge," and the deeply respected Sanhedrin became a lynch mob. The holiest city (Jerusalem) and the city of law (Rome) united to produce the greatest farce in legal history.

The only one in control was Jesus (John 10:17, 18; 19:10, 11). He had set His face to go to Jerusalem (Luke 9:51). His "hour" had come (John 17). Jesus forced His enemies to take action. He both provoked and facilitated His own arrest. Why can't we see this?

We have reduced Christ to a sweet, soft, nice baby Jesus. He is a Man among men, not a glorified weakling. He took on Satan, Judaism, and the whole world—and won. He never retreated from anybody!

Judaism (Jerusalem) was morally and spiritually

bankrupt. Seeing man at his worst, we see God at His best. This is the glory of grace. Jesus did not sneak into town or hide in a closet. He cleansed the temple (Mark 11:15–18). The Jews were so morally bankrupt that they were using the temple as a shortcut through Jerusalem. Jesus, alone, stopped that (Mark 11:16). What courage! What strength! In Jerusalem He taught "judgment parables." There is no neutrality with Jesus—you either accept Him or kill Him! His enemies never said, "Rebuke Him." They said, "Kill Him!"

The religious leaders were "scared out of their wits" of Jesus! His miracles could not be easily dismissed. Jerusalem was always hostile and unsympathetic to the truth about Jesus. Religious leaders had no control over Him or His ministry. Neither the Jews nor Pilate wanted a riot during the Passover. If the Jews had intended to kill Jesus during the feast, they would have made plans and not waited until Thursday night to implement them. This is where Judas entered the scene. Having been with Jesus and listened to His teachings in Jerusalem, he had heard Jesus announce His death. In one sense, this could be good news to His enemies, but the uncertainty during the feast panicked them. They had no fear of the fishermen and others who were His disciples, but they did not underestimate Jesus. They no longer denied the reality of His miracles. The Pharisees said, "Look, the world has gone after Him" (John 12:19b). It is true that the resurrection of Lazarus necessitated the death of Christ (John 11). Such truth and such miracles should terrify sinners! God gave the people of Jerusalem every opportunity to repent. They failed. The religious leaders lost not only their religious positions, but also their source of monetary gain (John 11:47, 48). No wonder Caiaphas announced that Jesus must die (John 11:49–53). "But the Jews were looking for a Messiah," you may say. Yes and no. They talked about it; they exploited it . . . but the last thing the religious leaders wanted was the Messiah. They knew He would put them "out of business." Pride, with power, does damnable things. Men with pride cannot give up power. They can only reject truth, fight truth, and try to destroy truth. The Jews, out of control, branded Jesus "guilty." Pilate and Herod (Rome) pronounced Him "not guilty" (Luke 23:12–16).

Among the most obvious irregularities in the trials of Jesus are these:

- The decision was made before the trial began.
- Officials had no authority to make an arrest at night unless someone was caught in the act of a crime. Judges were not to be part of an arrest.
- Capital trials could not be held at night. A criminal could not be acquitted in one day; a guilty verdict also demanded a night to think about it.
- Crucifixion was unknown to Jewish law.
- The judges were to be defenders as well as accusers.
- Hearsay evidence was inadmissible under Hebrew law.
- Circumstantial evidence was discredited; Hebrew law was based upon two or three witnesses. False witnesses were sought to testify against Jesus (Matthew 26:59–61).
- The youngest members of the Sanhedrin were to vote first.
- A member of the Sanhedrin was to be assigned to defend the accused.
- The Sanhedrin had no authority to originate charges . . . only to try them.

- Court sessions were forbidden on feast days and the eve of the Sabbath.
- The accused could not testify against himself.
- In trying capital crimes, the Sanhedrin was to meet only in the Hall of Hewn Stones.
- A high priest was not to rend his clothes.

The worst was done by those who supposed themselves to be the best. It is terrifying to think how monstrous men in sin can be!

THE JEWISH TRIALS

If not so contemptible, the arrest of Jesus would have been comical. The enemies of Jesus believed more in the power of Jesus than the disciples did. They sent a lynch mob (estimates range from 600 to 2,000 men) to arrest one unarmed preacher! Jesus, in plain view, had to help them.

He was first taken to Annas. This high priest had been ordained for life, but his corruption had ousted him and his sons. He was still the power. People with power need not have the title. Jesus was bounced back and forth like a ball between judges.

Annas sent Him to Caiaphas. This shows that Jesus was not on trial for religious reasons, but for the purposes of corrupt politics. Caiaphas, the son-in-law of Annas, was the high priest that year. It is humorous that Jesus' enemies could not even find paid false witnesses who would agree! Annas was powerful, feared, and hated. Caiaphas was but an "errand boy." Be a detective, and read Matthew 27:1, 2, 11; Mark 15:1, 2; Luke 23:1–3; John 18:29–33.

These men were unanimous in the one question that Pilate asked Jesus: "Are You the King of the Jews?" If a charge had not already been made, how did Pilate know what to ask? This suggests that someone had contacted Pilate earlier that night. Who could have gained access to Pilate that night? Probably, only the high priest, Caiaphas. Again, how could the tormenting dream of Pilate's wife make sense (Matthew 27:19)? This explains why the Jewish leaders were insulted when Pilate reopened the case. The Jews thought a deal had been made!

The Jewish leaders were proud, haughty, and conceited beyond words. They lost their composure. Barbarically, they spat on Jesus, slapped Him, punched Him, cursed Him, and taunted Him to prophesy blindfolded (Matthew 26:66–68; Mark 14:65; Luke 22:63–65). This is Hodge on the matter. I could endure curses and slaps, but *spit*? I do not think I could tolerate spit! How did God? Jesus prophesied spit (Mark 10:34; Luke 18:32). Jewish leaders spat in His face, and Roman soldiers spat on him (Matthew 26:67; 27:30; Mark 15:19). Disgusting! God's grace can even endure *spit*!

The Jewish supreme court was once praised as the Great Sanhedrin (seventy-one august members). Their illustrious position ended that day. Caiaphas, in desperation, forced Jesus to testify against Himself under oath (Matthew 26:62–64). Jesus not only accepted their accusation, but He even gave them further evidence to use against Him: "Nevertheless I tell you, hereafter you will see the Son of Man sitting at the right hand of Power, and coming on the clouds of heaven" (Matthew 26:64). With that, the Jews were infuriated!

THE ROMAN TRIALS
Pontius Pilate hated the Jews, and they hated him. They were stuck with each other, and each would do

anything to win. With his record of past mistakes, Pilate had to be very careful. The Jews wanted blood; Pilate wanted to save his political position.

The Jews exchanged the charge of blasphemy for one of political treason. Pilate tried to avoid being part of this travesty, yet he could not. He allowed others to judge, and they refused. He repeatedly declared Jesus "not guilty." He sent Jesus to Herod. Jesus did not acknowledge Herod's request for a magic show. He sent Jesus back to Pilate. The only thing achieved by this process was that Pilate and Herod became friends (Luke 23:12).

The Jews won, yet lost. They declared, "We have no king but Caesar" (John 19:15). They renounced God for Caesar. They bowed to that which they hated, even shouting, "His blood be on us and on our children!" (Matthew 27:25).

Pilate washed his hands; Jesus washed others' feet. What a difference!

Pilate marveled at the quiet composure of Jesus. Using Barabbas, he attempted to do a favor for the Jews. They rejected it! They chose Barabbas, a common thug! People will always choose a Barabbas.

Then Pilate had the "not guilty" Jesus crucified! This was the crime of crimes! Do not be prejudiced like the Jews, amused like Herod, or spineless like Pilate. The historian Eusebius[1] said that Pilate committed suicide. God wiped out Jerusalem (using Rome and Titus in A.D. 67–70). Do not mess with God!

The cross . . .
there is no other way!

---

[1] Eusebius *Ecclesiastical History* 2.7.

QUESTIONS FOR STUDY AND DISCUSSION

1. Why was Gethsemane such a struggle for Jesus?
2. What was the "big" sin that Judas committed?
3. Who was in control at the time of Jesus' arrest and His crucifixion? How do the Scriptures make this clear?
4. Using the Gospels, draw a timeline to track Jesus' trials. Point out the legal irregularities in the way these steps occurred.
5. Consider the roles of Annas, Caiaphas, and Pilate in the trials of Jesus. Why did they make the decisions they made?
6. What accusation did the Jews make against Jesus before Pilate?

3

"MORE CONFUSING THAN AMUSING"

CRUCIFIXION

"God forbid that I should glory, save in the cross of our Lord Jesus Christ." Crucifixion! How brutal, barbaric, cruel, and inhumane! Probably, it was invented by Persians and was later perfected by Romans. Rome became infamous for crucifixions. It was the ultimate form of humiliation. Animals today are not treated as Jesus was. Rome did not crucify Romans. The Jews despised crucifixion (Deuteronomy 21:23; Galatians 3:13); it was never their practice.

No word in the English language is more meaningful than the cross! We must approach the study of it with trembling. It must be a lifelong study for all Christians.

Modern civilization refuses crucifixion, yet parts of the world practice capital punishment. However, execution today is as quick and painless as possible.

Crucifixion stripped people of human dignity. Basically, crucifixion was used to kill a man and yet keep him alive as long as possible. In public view, a man was left naked (for all practical purposes), helpless, and open to abuse. Even with all this pain, men could live for days. Most lived two or three days. What horror! Oddly, there was not a great blood loss. No major arteries were affected. It was difficult to breathe. It was harder to exhale than to inhale. A man would push with his legs to breathe, which increased the pain from the nails. Death resulted primarily from hypovolemic shock and exhaustion as-phyxia. When the legs were broken, victims would die in a few minutes.

The word "excruciating" literally means "out of the cross." Movement multiplied misery. There was no com-fortable position on the cross. The pain was immense. Headaches, burning thirst, spasms of muscles and nerves—a million constant shocks were brought to the body. None of us has ever seen a crucifixion.

The scourging! Every Sunday we mention the cruci-fixion, but the cross does not shock us anymore. It must! Jesus prophesied His own suffering and scourging (Mat-thew 20:17–19; Mark 10:32–34; Luke 18:31–34).

Flogging was a legal preliminary in every Roman execution. It was brutal and inhumane. We cannot grasp the intensity of the Roman scourging. It produced great welts, deep stripes, and a swollen body. Often, eyes and teeth were knocked out. Some men died from it. Scourg-ing, however, was not for execution. The whip was for punishment; the nails were for death. Hardened, expe-rienced Roman soldiers knew when to stop.

Crucifixion could not be cheated by whipping. After the verdict, Pilate had Jesus scourged (Matthew 27:26; Mark 15:15; John 19:1). Pilate had hoped for sympa-thetic support and said, "Behold, the Man!" (John 19:5). This failed. Jesus did not get sympathy. Study and re-study Isaiah 53!

The Scriptures place little or no emphasis upon the pain and suffering! The Gospels avoid the horror as much as possible. Nothing is said about Jesus' crying. Sinners are not saved by pain, but by death. Still, the suffering is there. The cross was a silent death; victims did not have the strength or the breath to scream. The scourging was called the "little death"; crucifixion was the "big death."

The wounds! There are only five ways a person can be wounded. Jesus absorbed all five. (1) The contused wound involved bruises from fists and blunt instruments (Matthew 26:67; Mark 14:65; Luke 22:63). (2) The lacerated wound came with scourging. (3) The penetrating wound came from a sharp-pointed instrument. The soldiers crammed a crown of thorns upon His head (Matthew 27:29). (4) The perforated wound came when ". . . they pierced my hands and my feet" (Psalm 22:16). The hands could not bear the weight of the body. The nails went through His wrists, which are part of the hands. (5) The incised wound took place to make sure He was dead when a soldier pierced Jesus with a spear (John 19:34). The Roman soldiers would not leave the victim until they were sure of his death. The spear confirmed that Jesus was dead!

Six Hours, 1

Matthew 27:33–44; Mark 15:22–33;
Luke 23:32–43; John 19:15–27

"When they came to the place called The Skull, there they crucified Him and the criminals, one on the right and the other on the left" (Luke 23:33).

Six hours! Salvation . . . life . . . hope . . . heaven! Jesus was on the cross for six hours (Mark 15:25; Matthew 27:42–50; see Mark 15:30–37; Luke 23:44–46). The third hour until the ninth hour (Jewish time) is equivalent to 9:00 a.m. until 3:00 p.m. These six hours can be equally divided. God even did that. God sent utter darkness from the sixth to the ninth hours (Matthew 27:45; Mark 15:33; Luke 23:44). Jesus died at the ninth hour.

Do not try to embellish the cross. It needs no commentary. The only meritorious work in salvation is the cross. Some speak of "cheap grace," but there are no "cheap crosses." It is easy to be tolerant; it is difficult and costly to practice love.

The death of Jesus is the most famous death in all history. It is all that Christianity has, wants, or needs. Paul wrote, "For I determined to know nothing among you except Jesus Christ, and Him crucified" (1 Corinthians 2:2). This is all that Paul knew and all that he preached (1 Corinthians 1:17–25).

DETAILS NOT TOLD

We know so little! Details are few. John was the only apostle to witness the crucifixion, but he never opened his mouth. Luke (the historian) reduced the cross to one phrase in one verse: "There they crucified Him" (Luke 23:33b). We know more about His burial than His crucifixion. There are more questions than answers.

We do not know the shape of the cross. The cross shaped as an "X" is rejected. There is also the Tau cross, which looks like our capital "T." Since Pilate had a sign placed above Jesus' head, this, too, is eliminated. The Latin cross, shaped like a plus sign, is probably correct. It is the universal cross we widely accept in art, jewelry, and architecture. Anecdotally, it is called "the sign of the cross." Pilate wrote a sign to be placed above Jesus on the cross (Matthew 27:37; Mark 15:26; Luke 23:38; John 19:19). This sign can create problems. Each account is different, but they all say the same thing. The writers were not interested in the exact words, but in the message. Golgotha is ugly. Crucifixion is ugly. God did to His Son what we could never do. God poured out all of His holy anger upon Jesus; He hid His face from His Son.

How was Jesus nailed to the cross? We do not know. We do know that, once He was on the cross, onlookers jeeringly demanded that He come down (Matthew 27:39–43; Mark 15:29–32). The thieves being crucified joined in (Matthew 27:44; Luke 23:39). We also know that, as Jesus was dying for the sins of the world, soldiers gambled for His robe (Matthew 27:35; Mark 15:24; John 19:23, 24). How pathetic the cross is!

We know the day Jesus was resurrected: the first day, Sunday (Matthew 28:1; Mark 16:2, 9; Luke 24:1–7; John 20:1–10). There is no argument here. The early church assembled on that same day of the week (Acts 20:7; 1 Corinthians 16:2). *The day of the crucifixion is not named specifically.* To find that day, we must count backwards. Ten times the Gospels refer to Jesus' being raised on "the third day."[1] Some think He was crucified on Wednesday. The very idea of Wednesday eliminates itself. The Thursday theory also creates more problems than it claims to solve. The Bible teaches that He was raised on "the third day"—not "the fourth day" or "the fifth day." Throughout the centuries, Friday has been designated as the day of His death. Some even call it "Good Friday."

Jesus did speak of three days and three nights in relation to Jonah (Matthew 12:40)—but this was figurative, not literal. If He had spent three full days and nights in the tomb, the Resurrection would have been on "the fourth" or "the fifth" day. Man counts hours; the Bible simply refers to "the third day." From Friday, Sunday is the third day. The Jewish leaders knew this (Matthew 27:63). They asked Pilate to take action because they knew what Jesus had said. The apostles remembered this after His resurrection (Luke 24:8; John 2:18–22). They then understood what Jesus meant.

Unlike the gentle Jesus we have created in our minds, Jesus spoke harshly about Herod: "Go, tell that fox, 'Behold, I cast out demons and perform cures today and tomorrow, and *the third day* I reach My goal'" (Luke 13:32; emphasis mine). Although the timing is debated, we must understand that the Bible says the crucifixion day was the day before the Sabbath (the preparation day) (Mark 15:42; John 19:31; Luke 23:50–56).

---

[1]See Matthew 16:21; 17:23; 20:19; 27:63; Mark 9:31; 10:34; Luke 9:22; 13:32; 18:33; 24:7.

The crucifixion of Christ is so horrific that we tend to overlook or forget other shameless events leading up to it. Before that painful trip to Golgotha, Jesus appeared before Pilate a second time. Pilate could find no fault in Him. He offered to release Jesus and crucify Barabbas, but the Jews shouted, "Crucify, crucify!" (Matthew 27:15–23; Mark 15:6–13; John 18:39—19:6). Pilate then handed Him over to be crucified. The soldiers scourged Jesus and abused Him. They put a scarlet robe on Him for "sport." They placed a reed in His hand. They then crammed a crown of thorns upon His head (Matthew 27:27–31; Mark 15:15–20; John 19:1–3). They slapped Him and spat on Him. How mean man can be!

INTERRUPTIONS
ON THE WAY TO CALVARY

We usually try to avoid interruptions. Some can be painful. We usually think, "After this interruption, we can get back to life." No, no, no! Life is nothing but interruptions. The Gospels tell us about many interruptions in the life of Christ. As He made His way to Golgotha, we read of the interruption by Simon of Cyrene (Matthew 27:32, 33; Mark 15:21, 22; Luke 23:26). God's providence! This man had traveled hundreds of miles in the religious pilgrimage of a lifetime. Suddenly, he was commandeered to carry a prisoner's cross. Mark inserted an interesting footnote. Simon was the father of Alexander and Rufus. Paul saluted a Rufus in Romans 16:13. Consider the possibilities, but beware of your conclusions. Do not read into a Scripture what God has not written! Simon had no idea he would still be known today, after two thousand years. God blesses those who assist His Son. There were Cyrenians in Jerusalem on Pentecost

(Acts 2:10). There were preachers from Cyrene (Acts 11:20). Prophets from Cyrene were in the group called by God to start mission work (Acts 13:1–4). Cyrene looks like a good place in the Scriptures. We owe Simon a debt of thanks for carrying the cross. Jesus could barely stand. The pole for the cross was too big, heavy, and awkward to be carried. The part of the cross Simon carried was the crossbeam (crossbar). Thank you, Simon.

The next interruption involved sympathetic, heart-broken women (Luke 23:27–31). Jesus gave a frightening revelation. They were soon to cry over themselves. Men could kill God's Son, but they could not go unpunished for it. Jerusalem crucified Jesus; God allowed Jerusalem to be destroyed by Roman conquerors (A.D. 67–70). What about the women? They were there. They did not run. They cared. They looked on with love and devotion. The women watched Jesus' burial (Matthew 27:55, 56; Mark 15:47; Luke 23:49–56). They watched His tomb. May God bless our women!

Fellow Jews traded Jesus' life for that of a wretched crook, Barabbas. A trusted apostle, Judas, betrayed Him. His main apostle, Peter, denied Him. An illegal court sentenced Him. A bunch of bullies beat Him. Hardened soldiers crucified Him.

THE FIRST THREE HOURS

Six hours! The cross is the wedge in the center of time.

Immediately, Jesus was offered vinegar with gall (Matthew 27:34; KJV; Mark 15:23). Amazing! He did taste it, but then He rejected it. Jesus refused a painkiller. He did not want anesthetic. Jesus would keep His full senses upon the cross. He would not numb the pain at

41

the price of His faculties. Pain and agony were not issues at the cross. Jesus was the only person at the cross who was in control.

No sooner was He on the cross than the people chanted for Him to come down (Matthew 27:39–44; Mark 15:29–32; Luke 23:35–40). The thieves joined in also (Matthew 27:44; Mark 15:28, 32; Luke 23:39–41). What defiant cynicism! This demonstrated the ultimate depravity of unbelief, of disbelief. How dare man tell God the conditions on which he will believe! If Jesus had come down from the cross, sinners would have been damned to hell without hope. Jesus was born to die. He died that we might be born to live (Romans 5:10). God cannot forgive anyone without punishing the sin. At Calvary, Jesus bore the punishment for my sin.

Even forgiven sins have consequences. Jesus asked God not to count this sin against His tormentors; however, theirs was the sin of sins! God destroyed Jerusalem. In its biblical history, Judaism existed for one thing—the coming of the Messiah. Jesus came, fulfilling all those Messianic prophecies. They crucified Him! Ironically, this put them out of the "Messiah business." The Jews have not accepted the Messiah. They no longer teach about or expect the Messiah. Judaism today is an empty religion. The Jews rejected God as their King, accepting Caesar (John 19:14, 15). They fell further by placing Jesus' blood upon themselves and, to add to their sin, they put it upon their children (Matthew 27:25). The Jewish nation has become "a proverb and a byword" (1 Kings 9:7).

As Jesus was dying for the sins of all mankind, it was only fitting for Him to forgive a sinner. Study the exchange in Luke 23:39–43. A thief found true religion while being executed. Amazing! We must learn to count. We have one Lord, two thieves, three crosses, four garments, five wounds, *six hours*, and seven statements from Jesus. Study and restudy the cross. Come to the cross; stay at the cross. The cross saved the thief; the cross can save us! Man cannot be saved by ideas, thoughts, philosophies, mysticisms, or ignorance—man can only be saved by Jesus Christ!

Although dying in intense pain, Jesus took care of His mother. He told John to care for her as his mother (John 19:26, 27). Many think John "adopted" her for the rest of her life. Stop and think. Two of her sons wrote New Testament books (James and Jude). Mary and some of her sons were at the prayer service in the uppe r room in Jerusalem soon after Jesus' resurrection (Acts 1:13, 14). It is obvious they would take care of their mother's future needs. Mary needed help at the cross—right now, this minute! This was her hardest day, her longest night. Jesus was saying, "Stay with My mama!"

Every Jewish girl prayed to be the mother of the Messiah. Mary must have been thrilled to learn that God had chosen her (Luke 1:26–38). She also must have been intimidated. This was God's only begotten Son! What was it like to rear God's Son? Mary paid a tremendous price to rear Jesus. The aged prophet Simeon had blessed Joseph, Mary, and the baby Jesus. He had also told Mary that a sword would pierce her soul (Luke 2:34, 35). Mary was at that cross. That is how mothers are. Still, the cross was far from her understanding! She stood heartbroken and bewildered. Jesus comes to us, but at a price. Too many refuse to pay that price. Mary lovingly did.

Mary, now, is either banished or deified. Both are wrong. Although she was Jesus' mother, she had to be saved as all sinners do. She did not receive a divinely privileged position. She and the brothers of Jesus were redeemed by Jesus' blood the same way all others are. There was no fanfare for the family of Jesus. After Acts 1, Mary drops out of the Scriptures. Her Son also became her Savior!

The cross shouted to Mary as it shouts to us, "Life is not futile . . . failure is not fatal . . . death is not final!"

The cross . . .
there is no other way!

QUESTIONS FOR STUDY AND DISCUSSION

1. How do you think you would react if you actually witnessed a crucifixion?
2. Why was scourging called the "little death"?
3. Why does the cross need no commentary?
4. Why were so few details of the crucifixion recorded in the Scriptures?
5. Discuss the price that Mary paid as the mother of Jesus. What price must we pay as His followers?
6. What is the proper role of Mary in the New Testament church?
7. What statements did Jesus make while on the cross? What do these tell us about His state of mind?
8. Consider the terrible price that God and Jesus paid because of their love for us. What is your reaction to this love? How overwhelming is God's love to you? How grateful does His love make you?

4

"MORE CONFUSING THAN AMUSING"

THE HOLINESS OF GOD

"God forbid that I should glory, save in the cross of our Lord Jesus Christ." The text of 1 Peter 1:15, 16 says, "But like the Holy One who called you, be holy yourselves also in all your behavior; because it is written, 'You shall be holy, for I am holy.'" In studying the cross, we face the transcendent holiness of God! We are not to be as holy as God is; this is a burden no one could bear (Acts 15:10). God is "Holy, Holy, Holy" (Isaiah 6:3). He is not just "love, love, love" or "law, law, law." God is God, and I am not! Our first step down is when we lessen our faith in God. Do not bring God down to be like us. Lift yourself up to be like God. Sentimental ideas about God result in foolish blasphemy. God, today, is "in"; but the "in" God is not a holy God! People today seek to *feel* God while refusing to listen to God and know God (John 17:3).

God, in one sense, does not have attributes. He cannot be sliced up like pie. God is *"holy"*! Idols are not and cannot be holy! God's name is "Holy" (Isaiah 57:15). He is truly "Holy!" We need to recognize the "otherness" of God! He does not conform to a standard—He *is* that standard. God is an absolute, infinite, incomprehensible fullness of purity that is incapable of being other than what He is. The Spirit of God is the Spirit of truth. We must live in awe, in wonder of God Almighty! People

46

say, "Justice demands that God do this." No! Nothing and no one can make demands of God! God's being is unitary. He is not parts working together but simply *One*! God is never at cross-purposes with Himself. One attribute is not in conflict with another. God is not a "walking civil war."

Holiness is the unique characteristic of God which separates Him from His created beings and alleged gods. This allows God both to withhold His love and to give His love. No wonder the word "holy" is in the Bible more than six hundred times! Only a superior power can compel obedience. In all eternity nothing has entered God's Being, and nothing has been removed.

To reveal Himself, God uses anthropomorphisms, expressing His nature in human attributes. Holiness is the number one attribute and is explained by the others. God is love (1 John 4:8, 16), but love is not God. God defines love; love does not define God. Love cannot make sense apart from holiness. What holiness demands, love provides. If God is only equal to love, then the personality of God is destroyed. If all other attributes are denied except this one (love), then that one attribute becomes a substitute for God. Love is something true about God, but it is not God.

Holiness must be the business of every Christian! Why has holiness fallen upon hard times? Tragically, it has been orphaned by the church. No sermons, classes, or books are on holiness! Personal holiness has become obsolete. We do not even promote holiness in regard to Jesus. When was the last time you heard a sermon on "The Holiness of Jesus"? Holiness is not the way to Christ; Christ is the way to holiness. The Christian is not ruined by living in the world, but by allowing the world to live in him. Holiness is not only what God gives me, but also what I manifest in the life that God has given me. Holiness is a position, a practice, and a process.

People today exchange holiness for cheap, false spirituality. Spirituality can be faked or bragged about; holiness cannot. Can a person be proud of humility? Ironically, faithful brethren are totally unaware of having great virtues. Humble people deny their humility! In contrast, many people go to great lengths to promote their spirituality. One woman told me, "I am on a higher spiritual level than you are." I gave her two answers: (1) "I hope so," and (2) "How do you know?" Without holiness, we cannot see God (Hebrews 12:14). Our hearts are to be blameless in holiness before God (1 Thessalonians 3:12, 13). We are to perfect holiness in the fear of God (2 Corinthians 7:1), to be partakers of His holiness (Hebrews 12:10). We must revere holiness in order to accept or allow for wrath. We cannot appreciate or accept grace until we understand wrath. The question is not "How can a loving God send a sinner to hell?" but "How can a holy God *not* send a sinner to hell?"

Six Hours, 2

Matthew 27:45–50; Mark 15:33–37; Luke 23:44–46; John 19:28–30

"Therefore when Jesus had received the sour wine, He said, 'It is finished!' And He bowed His head and gave up His spirit" (John 19:30).

Six hours! Only Jesus' six hours on the cross can explain Pentecost (Acts 2). Three thousand baptisms took place, involving people from all over the known world. The speaker was an unknown preacher, Peter, who was not even a rabbi. He did not know that he was going to preach. He came without notes and was without his Bible. Nevertheless, this was the greatest response to a sermon in all of history. The most marvelous thing ever produced, the church, was accomplished on the cross.

God left nothing to chance. He is in complete control. Thousands of Jews had come to Jerusalem for Passover. For many, this was the religious pilgrimage of a lifetime. Some remained in Jerusalem for *fifty days* until Pentecost. People were crowded close together. All the talk was about the Passover and the empty tomb. There had never been a Passover like this one. God gave Israel fifty days to think about what had happened. Earthquakes had "rattled their teeth" (see Matthew 27:51–53). From the sixth hour to the ninth hour, God had sent darkness (Matthew 27:45; Luke 23:44, 45). God allowed the people to crucify Jesus, but He refused to let them enjoy seeing Him die. This time was spooky, weird, and scary! People were too scared to move, too afraid not to move. "What have we done?" was the question. Rocks were rent. Tombs were opened. Recognized folk from these opened tombs walked around after the resurrection (Matthew 27:51–54). As priests in the temple were serving (at the ninth hour), the veil was torn from top to bottom (Matthew 27:51; Mark 15:38; Luke 23:44, 45). Could this explain why many priests obeyed the gospel (Acts 6:7)? The euphoria that cried, "Crucify Him!" turned into hysteria. The participants were so scared that they smote their breasts. Even the Roman centurion recognized this as "from God" (see Matthew 27:54; Luke 23:47). For *fifty days* all that the people who had crowded into Jerusalem could see was an empty tomb. Pilate and the Jewish leaders knew that Jesus was resurrected. No search party was sent. The apostles were not questioned. The enemies knew before the disciples did. The apostles fled. Basically, they missed it. The women stayed (Matthew 27:55, 56; Luke 23:48, 49). They could not bear to watch, yet they refused to leave.

Christianity is built upon that staggering yet confusing empty tomb! The "empty tomb" is still empty. No tour guide at the Jerusalem cemetery will tell you, "This is where Jesus *is* buried. Here is His gravestone with His name on it." After Pentecost, that empty tomb went into oblivion. Read Acts 2. God came with a mighty wind. The Holy Spirit filled the apostles. Divided tongues as of fire sat upon them. Peter preached about what had happened *fifty days ago*! He said his listeners were not only witnesses but also perpetrators. He branded them murderers—murderers of God's Son! They were cut to their hearts. They cried out in terror. They repented. Three thousand were baptized. The church began in Jerusalem on Pentecost.

History reveals to us that "all the armies that ever marched, all the parliaments that ever sat, all the kings that ever reigned"[1] have not affected us as the one solitary life of Jesus Christ has. Those three thousand baptisms were no accident. Satan was not as smart as he thought he was. Do not underestimate Satan; do not overestimate Satan. Stop and think. Did he think he could kill God? Surely, he knew that, even if he did kill God, he could not keep God dead. Imagining that he had won, Satan defeated himself.

THE FINAL THREE HOURS

Six hours! The church is the only institution on earth that exists primarily for the benefit of those who are not members of it. Jesus did not use His divinity to escape His humanity. The final three hours were clothed in unnatural darkness. Quietness ruled. The only sounds anyone could hear were the groans of three dying men and the dropping of blood. What creepy darkness!

Grace and the gospel! Pride cannot allow grace; legalism can never understand grace. Grace is not something God forces upon sinners. Grace is an area, a container. The contents are accepted by faith and then utilized (Ephesians 2:4–10). Grace is not mystical but historical. God, in time, planted a cross. People of faith live in that sphere of grace. God's grace comes through our faith.

Six hours! In the final three hours, Jesus made four

---

[1]James Allan Francis, "Arise, Sir Knight," in *"The Real Jesus" and Other Sermons* (Philadelphia: Judson Press, 1926), 123–24.

more statements in quick succession. He cried, "Eli, Eli, lama sabachthani?" Interpreted, this means, "My God, My God, why have You forsaken Me?" (Matthew 27:46; Mark 15:34). God cannot touch sin, but God made Jesus to be sin (2 Corinthians 5:21). This is the only time in all eternity that God and Jesus were separated. How terrifying! Oh, the depth of sin! Do not minimize sin! Those near the cross thought Jesus was crying out for Elijah.

Separation from God was a deeper wound than any punishment man could inflict. This statement shouts out about the depth of man's fall, his lostness, and his helplessness. Jesus' death not only conquered sin, but it also conquered death (Hebrews 2:14–18). Christians no longer fear death. Satan is a defeated enemy; sin is a defeated curse. Death has lost its sting (1 Corinthians 15:21–26, 51–58).

Jesus, knowing that God's will was being done, allowed Himself to say, "I thirst." The humanity of Christ is seen in this, His sixth statement. Humanity's deepest cry is "I thirst" (John 19:28, 29; KJV). Cheap wine was handy. Even when something decent was done for Jesus, it was cheap. The "Water of Life" was thirsty! (John 6:51–58; Psalm 69:21). As a man, He said, "I thirst." Jesus was totally identified with humanity. He did not say, "I hurt." The writers of the Gospels avoided the pain and the agony. We are not saved by His pain; we are saved by His blood, His death.

Crucifixion was used to kill a man while keeping him alive as long as possible. Crucifixion took away all the rights of humanity. ". . . But everyone who saw him was even more horrified because he suffered until he no longer looked human" (Isaiah 52:14; CEV). The Jews had looked for the Messiah, but they rejected and crucified

Him when He came. What was their hope is now their death. Nothing can be more empty than a religion without a Messiah. God has not changed; God cannot change. Jesus, the Messiah, came. Then came the statement only Jesus could make: "It is finished!" (John 17:4, 5; 19:30). "The task is done!" God can be just while justifying sinners. Jesus said this to let us know how little we know! It is beyond our grasp! Heaven has to be eternal; it will take us all eternity to begin to grasp this. In heaven we will not be God (or gods). Heaven will be a learning experience. Being with God, we will further grasp His glory. Jesus will be there as "The Lamb" (as depicted in the entire Book of Revelation). All eternity will declare, "It is finished."

What man could not finish, Jesus did. The mouth of Satan (the accuser) was shut (Revelation 12:9–11). The old law of Moses was nailed to the cross. The new law of Christ came into effect (Hebrews 8:6–13; 9:12–18; 10:4–14, 18–31). The greatest mouthful ever said was "It is finished!"

Jesus made His last statement on the cross in a loud voice: "'Father, into Your hands I commit My spirit.' Having said this, He breathed His last" (Luke 23:46). Amazing! Jesus yelled! His crying out took great effort. He wanted all to hear this. Notice that He did not commend to God His body, His breath. He commended His spirit. Jesus, God's Son, had chosen to die!

THE GLORY OF THE CROSS

Six hours! Jesus never talked as much about being crucified as He did about being glorified. "Father, the hour has come; glorify Your Son, that the Son may glorify You"; "Now, Father, glorify Me together with Yourself, with the glory which I had with You before the world was" (John 17:1, 5). Our God turned the most inhumane instrument of execution into the greatest motivation! The cross is the magnetism of God. Do not talk about the God "within us" or "beside us" until you grasp the God "above us." God has two thrones—one in the highest heaven and the other in the lowest heart. You do not understand Christ until you understand the cross. The only person worthy of glory gave it all to His Father. Christians do not glory in anything but the cross (Galatians 6:14).

The cross . . .
there is no other way!

QUESTIONS FOR STUDY AND DISCUSSION

1. How can we say that God does not have "attributes"?
2. What is the difference between "holiness" and the popular understanding of "spirituality"?
3. Did God forsake Jesus while He was on the cross? Explain.
4. Review the last four recorded statements of Jesus while He was on the cross. What was the significance of each one?
5. Why is it important that Jesus' death not only conquered sin but also conquered death?
6. Why did so many obey the gospel on the Day of Pentecost?

5

"More Confusing Than Amusing"

The Appeal of the Cross

"God forbid that I should glory, save in the cross of our Lord Jesus Christ." The cross appeals to our understanding. By worldly standards the life of Christ was a failure. Rome was unchanged. Jerusalem was unchanged. When Jesus ascended, He left only 120 devout disciples (Acts 1:11–15). They were unknowns, penniless, without political power (Acts 4:13). However, when Peter and the eleven preached at Pentecost, about three thousand were baptized. Christianity came from an act in history. Christianity cannot be reduced to an idea, a philosophy, or a statement. It is a Person (Jesus Christ). It is not only what God said, but also what God did.

The "Golden Rule" is nice, but it cannot save. Salvation demands a cross. Sinners are not saved by personal attainment, but by cross attainment. Salvation only comes from doctrinal truth, not personal growth. Nothing on earth is as powerful as the cross of Christ. The simplest mind can understand an historical act (2 Corinthians 5:17–21). Culture tries to offer Christ without a cross. Communism offers a cross without a Christ. One is religion without sacrifice; the other is sacrifice without religion. Both fail! Having been taken to the cross, no one can remain the same.

The cross appeals to our deepest emotions. The cross is God's "plus" sign for all the world is the "minus" of.

Jesus said, "'And I, if I am lifted up from the earth, will draw all men to Myself.' But He was saying this to indicate the kind of death by which He was to die" (John 12:32, 33). The cross stirs our indignation; the cross stirs our admiration. The cross breaks our hearts. The cross compels, impels, and propels. A heart without the cross is a mission field; a heart with the cross is a missionary. Evangelism lives in a cross-centered heart. Salvation escapes those who think they can save themselves. There is no end to the cross. Every day there is something new, different, and poignant. It is unthinkable that sinners could glory.

The cross appeals to our human dignity. God could have coerced; instead, He invites. In this one sense, He is at our mercy. God does not bully. People are drawn by the magnet of the cross. The closer you get, the more powerful it is. You tremble; you cry; you shout! Empathy, sympathy, anger, and joy! The cross can only be received and preached with passion. Salvation is not a business transaction. Scheming Caiaphas, cowardly Pilate, and heartless Herod have all been judged by history. Who won? Jesus Christ! No "myth" can change a person. Jesus changes people. Paul called this the "mystery of godliness" (1 Timothy 3:16). The most intriguing thing about Christianity is the cross.

The cross appeals to our sense of moral obligation. No one can remain neutral at the foot of it. Nothing we can do by ourselves has any worth! Jesus draws—not drives—people to God (John 6:44–47). We fail in conversion when we try to push, intimidate, or manipulate people. In whatever age the cross finds itself, it is always out of place. Extravagant, ugly, unmanageable, and grotesque—the cross has never been popular, and it never will be.

Still, it is the greatest story ever told!

Living for Jesus a life that is true,
Striving to please Him in all that I do;
Yielding allegiance, glad-hearted and free,
This is the pathway of blessing for me.

Living for Jesus who died in my place,
Bearing on Calv'ry my sin and disgrace;
Such love constrains me to answer His call,
Follow His leading and give Him my all.

Living for Jesus thru earth's little while,
My dearest treasure, the light of His smile;
Seeking the lost ones He died to redeem,
Bringing the weary to find rest in Him.

O Jesus, Lord and Savior,
I give myself to Thee,
For Thou in Thy atonement,
Didst give Thyself for me;
I own no other Master,
My heart shall be Thy throne;
My life I give, henceforth to live,
O Christ, for Thee alone.[1]

---

[1]T. O. Chisholm, "Living for Jesus," *Songs of Faith and Praise*, comp. and ed. Alton H. Howard (West Monroe, La.: Howard Publishing Co., 1994).

Statements at the Cross

Matthew 27; Mark 15; Luke 23; John 19

"But Jesus was saying, 'Father, forgive them; for they do not know what they are doing'" (Luke 23:34a).

Nothing reveals God like the cross; nothing exposes man like the cross. The cross is ugly and grotesque; only God could glorify a cross. Crucifixion was chaos, profanity, cries, pain, and venom. You would not expect profound philosophy to be there, yet some of the greatest statements in all history were made there. Common men know them still today. Of seven statements that Jesus made while on the cross, the first three focused on others; the final four concerned Himself. The statements were brief. Even one word said it all—*"Tetelestai."* ("It is finished!")

STATEMENTS BY JESUS
(1) *Forgiveness.* "Father, forgive them; for they do not know what they are doing" (Luke 23:34). This was a prayer, not a declaration. Jesus' first and last statements were prayers to His Father. In our culture, forgiveness is "in," but the popular idea that God will simply "get us out of trouble" is ludicrous. Biblical forgiveness cannot be given without a repentance that leads to reconciliation.

59

Contrary to what some teach today, Jesus did not shout, "I forgive you." Prayer was rare on crosses. To pray for the executioners was unthinkable. However, this is what Jesus did. In dying on the cross, Jesus had to activate His own pure heart. He was praying for forgiveness for those who were committing the crime of killing God's Son. Heinous! Some scholars think Jesus repeated this statement throughout His hours of suffering on the cross. Think about this! The cross is forgiveness.

(2) *Salvation.* ". . . today you shall be with Me in Paradise" (Luke 23:43). The first two statements were for the crowd in general and the thief in particular. The penitent thief would be with Jesus! Was this thief more lost than we are? Sin-soaked sinners are saved by a blood-stained Savior! Jesus had power on earth to forgive sin (Matthew 9:6; Mark 2:10; Luke 5:23, 24). Isaiah said that Jesus would be numbered with the transgressors. He was crucified between two thieves. It seems that it is easier for God to convert the "unrighteous" than the "self- righteous."

(3) *Responsibility.* "Woman, behold your son!" (John 19:26, 27). The "woman" was Jesus' mother, Mary. John was the "son." Jesus had just called God "Father." To call Mary "Mother" could be perverted into beatification. Tragically, some religions do that.

Can you remotely grasp how it was to live in the house with Jesus? It is easier to grasp His divinity than His humanity. A young Jewish girl was called by God to bear and rear His Son (Luke 1:26–33). Humanly speaking, we might think that Jesus would have been an "A" student, a star athlete, the young man voted "most likely to succeed." "What then will this child turn out to be?" Mary wondered (see Luke 1:66).

Of all people, who will be with you, no matter what? Your mother! Friends like Peter deny, and sheep will scatter; but mothers will always be there! Jesus could not abort His cross, but He could provide for His mother. Only a mother can remotely know how Mary felt. Were the brothers of Jesus there? Were His sisters? No one knows, but mothers are always there. Simeon, the prophet, had tersely said, "A sword will pierce even your own soul" (Luke 2:35). Mary paid a price to rear Jesus. Discipleship costs.

What is the lesson here? Family does not count. God is not partial (Acts 10:34). Mary, Jesus' brothers, and His sisters had to obey the gospel as others did! They were present in the prayer session before Pentecost (Acts 1:13, 14). Joseph, the adopted father, just disappeared in the Gospels. Mary did the same in the Epistles. Two of her sons, James and Jude, wrote books of the Bible.

Jesus saw His mother. In no measure could she grasp the cross. He forgot His own pain to care for His mother, saying, "John, take care of her." This was not permanent. It was necessary that day. James and Jude would take care of their mother!

(4) *Pathos*. "My God, My God, why have You forsaken Me?" (Matthew 27:46). Jesus' first three statements on the cross concerned others. The final four concerned Jesus and the Father.

My parents were married seventy-one years and died two weeks apart. Their lives were so intertwined that they could not live separated. God was merciful. That moment at the cross was the only time in all eternity that God and Jesus were separated. No wonder Jesus was sorrowful, even unto death (Matthew 26:38, 39). As a young preacher, I encouraged grieving mates by saying,

"They are better off." I do not do that anymore! The loss of a tenured mate is life's greatest loss. When one dies, both die in certain ways.

God did not abandon Jesus; He abandoned sin! Sinners who forsake God are forsaken by God. Jesus called upon God twice. God was being God. There is a great mystery to the cross. His statement is a quotation from Psalm 22:1.

As usual, man missed the point. The people thought Jesus was calling for Elijah! They were cruel, making sport of it all. Jesus did not fear nails or death, but He did shudder at the loneliness of being made sin. How horrifying! Jesus was made to be everything that God hates, and He had to suffer through this *alone*! Jesus never defended Himself. This is the depth of His vicarious death. If Jesus had saved Himself, He could not save us. If He was to save us, He could not save Himself. He could not do both.

(5) *Thirst.* "I thirst" (John 19:28; KJV). This was another Scripture fulfilled (Psalm 69:21). At this point, Jesus spoke four times in quick succession. It is arresting to me that not every statement made by Jesus on the cross was recorded in every Gospel Account. Basically, one writer revealed what the others did not.

Jesus kept His full senses upon the cross. He first refused to drink to keep His senses. Then He did drink to keep His senses. He had complete control upon the cross. Of all the pains and discomforts He experienced upon the cross, this is the only one He mentioned. This was the only physical statement Jesus made upon the cross. It was the only personal favor He requested. This little statement is power-packed with thought. A dying man's final statements haunt us. They should. Only when knowing He had fulfilled His task (John 19:28) did Jesus ask for this personal favor.

(6) *Victory.* "It is finished!" (John 19:30). Jesus said this that we might know how little we know. Only Jesus, with one word (*tetelestai*), could sum up the entire scheme of redemption! Heaven must be eternal. It will take all eternity for us to grasp our salvation! He is the only person who fully did what God wanted done. He claimed victory before it was fully done! *Tetelestai!* ("It is finished!": three words in English but one in Greek.) This is the greatest single word ever said. Jesus came to do God's will. He did it! Man, lost in sin, now has a Savior. *Hallelujah!*

(7) *Faith.* "Father, into Your hands I commit My spirit" (Luke 23:46). Jesus did not die in doubt. He died in joyous faith! Yes, man in a human sense killed Jesus, yet in another sense man did not. Jesus chose when He would die and when He would be resurrected. "No one has taken it [My life] away from Me, but I lay it down on My own initiative. I have authority to lay it down, and I have authority to take it up again" (John 10:18). Jesus told Pilate that his power was only allowed by God (John 19:10, 11). The spirit of Jesus was not taken from Him; He voluntarily gave it to the Father. How Jesus lived! How Jesus died! This also fulfilled a Scripture (Psalm 31:5). Jesus, the Word, respected "the Word." We must learn this!

Jesus cried loudly in triumph! There is a time to yell, to cry loudly. Let us never preach the cross without passion!

STATEMENTS BY OTHERS

(1) *"Come down."* "If You are the Son of God, come down from the cross" (Matthew 27:39, 40). Jesus' tormen-

tors no sooner had Him on the cross than they wanted Him to come down: ". . . come down from the cross, so that we may see and believe!" (Mark 15:32). Believing is not at all what they would have done. If Jesus had come down from the cross, they would have put Him back on it! People with demands cannot and will not believe. Stubborn sinners cannot believe. No one could deny that Lazarus had been resurrected (John 11). This resurrection precipitated Christ's death. Enemies did not deny Peter's miracle (Acts 4:13–17). Miracles are not the power for faith!

We all find ourselves at the cross. What a motley group we see there: enemies, the curious, the ignorant, spectators, the scared disciples, and the loved ones! Jesus was the only one under control.

(2) *Change.* "Remember me" (Luke 23:42). One thief was impenitent. The cross either makes men better or worse. The selfish life of one thief ended in his selfish death. The other thief repented. The penitent thief was the only man on earth who had a clue about what was happening. He realized that he had lived a wicked life. The gospel must be "bad news" before it can be "good news."

(3) *Magic.* "Are you not the Christ? Save Yourself and us!" (Luke 23:39). "Amaze us with a trick." Jesus is not a magician. There is a sense in which no one is as unsensational as God! Men crave excitement. Even at the cross, they could not just sit beneath it. They tried to do something. Everything they said and did failed. Tragically, brethren today promote excitement. They want "holy goose bumps." They hear with their eyes and think with their feelings. It is easy to be tolerant; it is very difficult to practice love. The impenitent thief was guilty

of many crimes, even blasphemy (Luke 23:39). He was brazen. How could a dying thief be demanding?

It is tragic when the church is unable to change the world. It is hopeless when the church becomes worldly.

Man would rather die than think. He is his own worst enemy. What if Jesus had saved Himself? This would have doomed man. Jesus could not save *both* Himself and us.

(4) *Gawkers.* "Let us see whether Elijah will come to save Him" (Matthew 27:47–49; see Mark 15:36). Gawkers are dangerous. After Jesus cried aloud to God, bystanders did what bystanders do—they mixed up everything! Hearing a cry from the depths of Jesus' heart, superstitious man confused Elijah with God. Bystanders (thrillseekers) see everything and still miss everything. They see all that happens and understand nothing. All that bystanders offered Jesus was vinegar! What a travesty!

(5) *Gamblers.* "Let us not tear it, but cast lots for it" (John 19:24). Jesus was dying for our sins; men were gambling for His clothes. Do not gamble with the cross. The tragedy in life is not just what men suffer, but also what men miss! All of us are selling our lives for something. A man can gain the whole world and lose his soul (Matthew 16:24–26). Men gambled while God was saving them! Men were more interested in the worth of a robe than the life of a man. Things were more important than people. Are we any different? Are we any better? We know the price of everything and the value of nothing. Jesus went back to heaven; what happened to that robe?

(6) *Too little, too late.* Joseph of Arimathea and Nicodemus asked boldly for Christ's body (John 19:38–40;

Luke 23:50–53). We do appreciate them, for they buried Jesus. However, Jesus never asked that of them. Too many people think the way they did. Joseph and Nicodemus thought they were assets. God does not need assets; He only wants servants. Too many only want to serve God in an advisory capacity. Two men who could have done so much did so little! They only claimed the dead body of a man they had rejected when He was alive. Jesus asks us for our lives; we are only willing to perfume His body! Their action did take nerve, but it takes true courage to confess Jesus, to make Jesus who He is— Lord.

(7) *Conclusion time.* "Truly this man was the Son of God" (Mark 15:39). This was just another bloody day for this jaded centurion, but perhaps he took pride in his job and did it well. He watched every movement; he heard every word. Jesus was different. This cross was different. Unknowingly, this honest man immortalized himself. What the world, the crowds, and the enemies totally missed, this man saw! This is the only conclusion. Jesus is the Son of God, or He is not! The centurion made his decision; we must make ours!

The cross . . .
there is no other way!

QUESTIONS FOR STUDY AND DISCUSSION

1. How does the cross appeal to our emotions?
2. How does the cross appeal to our human dignity and moral obligation?
3. List the statements Jesus made while on the cross. What can we learn from each one?
4. Consider statements made by those who were watching the crucifixion. What comments might you have made?
5. Why did listeners think Jesus was calling for Elijah? What did they expect to happen?
6. What impact did the crucifixion have on the various onlookers?

6

"MORE CONFUSING THAN AMUSING"

THE MYSTERY OF THE CROSS

"By common confession, great is the mystery of godliness: He who was revealed in the flesh, was vindicated in the Spirit, seen by angels, proclaimed among the nations, believed on in the world, taken up in glory" (1 Timothy 3:16).

"God forbid that I should glory, save in the cross of our Lord Jesus Christ." The word "mystery" is a mystery. "Mystery" is not to be understood as "mysterious" (as is the case with mystical ecstasies, vibrations, the occult, or hobgoblins). Mystery and superstition have nothing in common. People love the magical, the bizarre, and the sensational. We are more interested in teasing our curiosity than living meaningful lives. God gives us the right kind of mystery in the gospel. The simple and divine things are always a mystery (such as marriage; Ephesians 5:20–33).

We say more than we understand. "Mystery" does not refer to something we need a detective to investigate. It is not the absence of meaning, but a greater meaning than we can comprehend. The fact that you cannot fully understand something does not mean that you cannot understand it at all. No one can fully grasp love, faith, justice, or goodness.

The cross is the greatest mystery of God. A little child can drink of it; old men can chew on it. Still, men do not know even a "thimbleful" about it. A thing not explained does not mean it is "unexplainable." Mystery challenges and allows growth. Creeds cannot contain mysteries. A mystery defies our grasp and is difficult to communicate. Eternal principles are larger than human words. We think we know who we are, but we do not! We have daily surprises that result in our saying, "I never understood this!" Sinful man is always strong in things that do not matter but weak in eternal things that do matter. We do not conquer mystery—we use it, grow in it, and celebrate it.

Mystery is understood only by revelation, not by reason. God can be known but not figured out. You cannot understand grace until you accept wrath. Until you understand the cross, you cannot understand Christianity. Where there is no mystery, there is no wonder. Without wonder, there is no real worship. When you explain magic, nothing is left; when you understand mystery, there is everything! Mysteries are not discovered in Eastern religion or Western logic. Mystery comes only by divine revelation. A mystery is an eternal secret that can be disclosed by God alone. A truth once hidden is now revealed. The secret things belong to God . . . but they are revealed to us. You do not have to be "one of the initiated" or know the "secret handshake."

Paul said that the gospel is a mystery (Ephesians 6:19). Faith is a mystery (1 Timothy 3:9) to be lived in a pure conscience. Redemption in Christ is the mystery that saves and unites Jews and Gentiles (Ephesians 1:7–13). Paul said this truth about Christ had been kept secret since the world began (Romans 16:25, 26; 1 Corinthians 2:7). This mystery was "for obedience to the faith" (Romans 1:5; NKJV). The mystery by revelation tells us what to believe and what to obey. This mystery of grace was revealed by the Spirit through His holy apostles and prophets (Ephesians 3:2–6). This truth, this unity, previously had not been made known. Paul also referred to "Christ and the church" as a "great mystery" (Ephesians 5:32). He used this description in regard to husbands and wives and the depth of marriage (Ephesians 5:21–33). All the beautiful, great things in life involve mystery.

One of the great revelations is found in Ephesians 3:9–11. God created all things in and for Christ. God planted a cross in His mind and heart before the creation. His plan was fulfilled by Christ on the cross. His blood purchased the church (Acts 20:28). Now, the manifold wisdom of God is displayed only in Christ by His church. This is God's eternal purpose. Mystery requires obedience without full knowledge. Simply trust and obey! We must know enough not to deny what we cannot understand.

Great living demands a mystery! Our deepest passion must focus upon things too wonderful to be fully understood.

I have nothing to offer God . . . but *thirst*!

People at the Cross

Matthew 27; Mark 15; Luke 23; John 19

"But standing by the cross of Jesus were His mother, and His mother's sister, Mary the wife of Clopas, and Mary Magdalene" (John 19:25b).

Study the Bible as a detective. Try to put the pieces together even if you do not have all the pieces. Beware. Be honest. Exercise caution! Be careful of the translation you "like" when teaching a verse. Do not try to make the Bible say what it has not said.

Your judgment of biblical characters is more a judgment of yourself. Great teachings come from people at the cross. Equally great teachings come from people *not* at the cross. Keep your eyes wide open. Unanswered questions are not as dangerous as answers to questions that God does not ask.

SOME WHO WERE ABSENT

The apostles. Eleven of the twelve were not there. Only John went the entire distance . . . yet he never said a word. Jesus deserved better! Would we have done better? Jesus could still forgive and use the apostles. This gives me hope! They simply fled (Zechariah 13:7; Matthew 26:56; Mark 14:50). Faith believes that God knows what He is doing! Was the cross too much for the apostles? Did the pain and agony overcome them? The Bible does not stress the suffering. It emphasizes the blood, the death, and the resurrection.

Mary, Martha, and Lazarus. These three are not mentioned at the cross, at the tomb, or in the upper room (Acts 1:13, 14). They are not listed in Acts or in the Epistles. These were the people with whom Jesus spent His final days. He loved them (John 11:5).

It has always amazed me how people (family, friends, and enemies) thought they could rebuke Jesus! Preaching humbles us. Many times, you have the least influence over those you love and those to whom you devote the most effort. Had they already hurt too much (John 11:1–44)? It has been said that the resurrection of Lazarus precipitated the crucifixion of Jesus. A price has to be paid to follow Jesus.

Others. Were the physical brothers of Jesus there? They were in the upper room in Acts 1, but they were not at their mother's side at the cross. John was (John 19:25–27). Was Barabbas there? We would call him a terrorist (John 18:39, 40). Pilate was shocked that the Jews chose to release Barabbas rather than Jesus (Matthew 27:15–22; Mark 15:6–13). What do you think he should have done? What about the many people Jesus had healed? Were they there? Were the people of Nazareth there? Were they too embarrassed or too ashamed?

What about Malchus? God in His Bible gave nearly as much space to Malchus as to the initial creation of things (John 18:1–11). God went into great detail: We know his name, his owner, his position, which ear was severed (the right one). Jesus' "motley crew" had two swords (Luke 22:38). In Gethsemane He and His apostles were confronted by a well-armed lynch mob (John 18:3). When Jesus said, "I am He," the mob drew back and fell to the ground (John 18:4–8). Amazing! Humorous! A hostile crowd sent to arrest one peaceful preacher!

When you do not know what to do, it is best to do nothing. Peter did not think of that. He pulled out his sword and cut off the right ear of Malchus!

Think. Stage this scenario! How could right-handed Peter, swinging his sword wildly, have cut off the right ear of Malchus? Impossible! Panic in the crowd could have brought death to Jesus and His group in two minutes. Peter knew how to use his sword. He knew upon whom he could use it (Malchus, a slave, not an official). He was saying, "You can kill us, but some of you will die too." When Jesus told him to put away his weapon, Peter settled down. Jesus calmly restored the ear. There was no panic.

Here we witness the sovereign majesty of Jesus! The miracle could not be denied. The humor cannot be overlooked. Caiaphas, the high priest, had to see that ear every day. It is amazing how Jesus guarded all His apostles (John 17:12). Do not criticize Peter either. He was willing to take on the entire Roman army.

Judas was not there because he was dead! His story is the worst of the worst! God does not think or act like man. No one demonstrates this more than Judas. His name sends shudders up and down our spines. Some suggest that God rejected him and that is why he betrayed Jesus. This denigrates God. God does not misuse or abuse people. New interpretations give Judas a lofty cause! This cannot be! In listing the apostles, the Scriptures always name Peter first and Judas last. He allowed Judas to approach Him, even to kiss Him (Luke 22:47, 48). He was still saying, "Don't do this—run, Judas, run." Jesus chose Judas, and Judas chose Jesus. Jesus knew that he was a devil (John 6:70, 71). He called him the "son of perdition" (John 17:12). John said that Judas, the trusted treasurer, was a crook who stole from the apostles' money bag (see John 12:1–6). Critics of the Scriptures never learn. They claim that Judas will be saved because he cooperated with God by betraying Jesus!

Judas was a successful hypocrite. The eleven did not have a clue what he was doing. They said, "Is it I?" not "It is Judas" (Matthew 26:21–25). Even after telling them about the "sop," the apostles still did not know (John 13:21–26). However, Judas knew—and Jesus knew!

Satan "entered" Judas (Luke 22:3; John 13:2). A man made for God can be used by Satan. Jesus told him to act quickly (John 13:26–30). He went to the priests. As a disciple, he was disloyal to his teacher. He betrayed Jesus for only a few dollars. Notice . . . he went to the priests, not the Pharisees. The other apostles would have killed him if they had known what he was about to do. They did not know his heart by his outward appearance. He had no horns or pitchfork.

Few men were as blessed as Judas. He was with Jesus for three years. He had special privileges, yet he failed to benefit from them. He could not learn; he could not admit error; he could not repent. To be blunt, Judas could not accept grace. Peter could! Judas had regret from pride, not repentance from grace. No man was ever as warned as Judas. Months before the betrayal, Jesus said, "Did I Myself not choose you, the twelve, and yet one of you is a devil?" (John 6:70). Judas could have been forgiven, but not restored as an apostle. This sin forbade the brethren to accept him. Judas feared life more than death. He committed suicide—a permanent solution to a temporary problem.

What is the lesson for us? If Jesus cannot save all, neither can we! Jesus summed it up tersely: "It would have been good for that man if he had not been born" (Matthew 26:24b).

SOME WHO WERE PRESENT

The women. The women were there. Where were the men? Mary, the mother of Jesus, was there. Mothers will always be there. She could not understand. Neither can we. Mary Magdalene was there. Jesus, after His resurrection, appeared first to Mary Magdalene, from whom He had cast out seven demons (Mark 16:9). There was a third Mary, the mother of James and Joses (Mark 15:40). Also, Salome, the mother of James and John, was at the cross, as was Joanna (Luke 24:10; 8:3). The women from Galilee (John 19:25; Matthew 27:56; Mark 15:40–47; Luke 23:49, 55, 56; 23:27–31) stayed nearby. Jesus stopped while approaching Golgotha to bless and encourage them. Women were last at the cross and first at the tomb. Praise God for women!

The thief on the cross (Luke 23:39–43). The thief fascinates us. In any debate concerning salvation, I bring up the thief first! Nothing exposes how we think like the thief. Quickly, you learn if your opponent is willing to think and to be honest. Some become brain-dead; others become heartless. Do not abuse the thief to promote your ideas. Think! Be honest!

The thief was saved. The thief—along with others like him—was the reason Jesus went to the cross. As Jesus was dying to save *all* sinners, it was natural for Him to save a sinner beside Him. Jesus died *with* sinners *for* sinners. While on earth, Jesus had the power to forgive sin (Matthew 9:4–6; Mark 2:8–11; Luke 5:23, 24). Jesus was dying, but He was not dead. Some cry, "The thief was too bad, too fallen, too late, and too far gone." Do not tell God how to dispense His grace! Do not tell Jesus whom He can save! Why try to keep any sinner lost? The greatest day in this man's life was his crucifixion!

"But he did nothing," you say. Wrong! He claimed the moment. He did what he could. He confessed Jesus as Lord. He rebuked the impenitent thief. He was the only person who defended Christ on the cross. "He was saved without baptism," you say. Beware! The thief exposes our thinking and our level of honesty. No one knows whether or not the thief was baptized, since sinners obeyed John the Baptist's baptism (Matthew 3:4–6; Mark 1:4, 5). Religious folk rejected both John and his baptism (Luke 7:29, 30). Publicans and harlots accepted John's baptism. Jesus and His apostles, later, were baptizing more people than John was (John 4:1, 2). John thundered at the Pharisees and the Sadducees because of their rejection (Matthew 3:7–12). The circumstances suggest that the thief *could* have been baptized. Do not gamble your soul upon a thief who may not have been baptized. Never draw an eternal conclusion from an assumption.

The thief died under the law of Moses, but we live under the law of Christ (Galatians 6:2). When the thief died, Jesus had not been raised from the dead; He had not given His Great Commission (Matthew 28:18–20; Mark 16:15, 16). The Holy Spirit had not come; people had not been commanded to be baptized to become Christians. The church had not been established (Pentecost, Acts 2:36–37). No one can be saved today as the thief was!

Under severe humiliation and excruciating pain, the thief did his best thinking. He rebuked the other thief for blasphemy. He confessed their guilt. He defended Jesus. He used "kingdom language." To some degree, he glimpsed the resurrection. Both the thief and Jesus were dying. Only a great miracle or resurrection could offer any future hope. He did not try to manipulate Jesus as the other thief did. In his helplessness, he threw himself down before "the mercy of the court." This, in no way, is "deathbed salvation." The thief confessed his faith in Jesus, and he who deserved hell got heaven.

Simon of Cyrene (Matthew 27:32; Mark 15:21; Luke 23:26). The humanity of Jesus failed. He could carry the cross no farther. Simon was told to carry the cross to Golgotha. Whatever his thoughts and motives were, his name will forever be in the Bible and in history. Many identify him as a Christian connected with Simeon (Acts 13:1) and Rufus (Romans 16:13).

The crowds (Matthew 26:65–68; Mark 14:64, 65; 15:29–36). Gawkers walked by, watching and ridiculing those being crucified. Crosses brought out the inhumanity in man. To spectators this was a sport—an ugly, bloody game. Experiments were encouraged. "Come down. . . ." "Stay put. . . ." "Give Him some cheap vinegar. . . ." "Maybe Elijah will come!" What a show! Today, the world is filled with protesters. Where were the protesters when they were needed? "His blood shall be on us and on our children!" the crowd had cried (Matthew 27:25). What a terrible price to pay!

The enemies. With pride they said, "That took care of that!" However, Sunday was coming. They set their own trap. Christianity stormed throughout the world. Biblical Judaism ended. Genealogies ceased. Jerusalem was sacked in A.D. 70. No one can fight against God and win.

Roman soldiers. Barbaric events demand barbaric people. The soldiers dressed Jesus as royalty and then had a party (Matthew 20:17–19; 27:27–31; Mark 10:32–34; 15:16–20; Luke 18:31–34; John 19:1–6). Jesus was beaten severely. Many died from such scourging. The soldiers gambled for His clothes (Matthew 27:35; Mark 15:24; John 19:23, 24). This added insult to injury. One Roman centurion watched intently. He saw that Jesus was different. He concluded, "Truly this was the Son of God!" (Matthew 27:54; see Mark 15:39; Luke 23:47).

The cross . . .
there is no other way!

QUESTIONS FOR STUDY AND DISCUSSION

1. What is the dictionary definition of "mystery"? What is the biblical meaning?
2. Explain why the gospel is called a "mystery."
3. Who was noticeably absent from the cross when Jesus was crucified? Why?
4. According to the Scriptures, how should we view Judas' role in betraying Jesus?
5. Consider those who were at the cross. Why were they there? What relationships did they have with Jesus? How did the crucifixion impact them?
6. Discuss the thief on the cross who was saved. How are we like him? How was his situation different from ours concerning salvation?

7

"More Confusing Than Amusing"

The Wisdom and Power of God

"God forbid that I should glory, save in the cross of our Lord Jesus Christ." "Christ [is] the power of God and the wisdom of God" (1 Corinthians 1:24; read 1:17—2:5). This defines Jesus as Lord. Christianity is Christ. Our power is in God's message, not man's method. You can only build your life upon Christ. Christianity is radical and demanding. Man does face-lifts and makeovers; God only does heart transplants. Christianity is a Person, not a program. There can be no tragedy worse than Christians living so that others cannot tell the difference between Christians and sinners. Our sinful lives can cause the gospel to be emptied of its power (1 Corinthians 1:17; NIV). Christianity makes a person a new creation with a new life and mind (2 Corinthians 5:17; John 3:1–7; Galatians 2:20, 21; Philippians 2:5–11). Jesus calls us to die.

The cross made everything "topsy-turvy." You die to live, and you give to get. The way up is down; the last shall be first. A crucified God is an oxymoron. Only God would take an instrument of execution (the cross) and make it the greatest motivation upon earth. Apart from the cross, there is no power to die to self. Jesus said, "And I, if I am lifted up from the earth, will draw all men to Myself" (John 12:32). People want life—the cross offers death as the way to life. People crave victory—the cross is a defeat that leads to victory. People want comfort—the cross is humiliation that opens the door to forgiveness. People want peace—the cross brings us to a war that results in peace. People honor beauty—the cross, crude and ugly, expresses a beauty that excels all other beauties. If you wish for the power and wisdom of God, you begin with Christ upon a cross.

CHRIST, THE POWER OF GOD

What kind of God would save sinners with a cross? (Romans 1:16). Our world worships brute power. God's power is greater than all other powers combined. It is awesome. He created and upholds the world by His Word (Genesis 1; 2; Hebrews 1:3). God's greatest strength can only be revealed in weakness! God does not force His way into our lives—He stands at the door and knocks (Revelation 3:20). This is the risk, the humility of God. You cannot make anything grow by pounding it with a sledgehammer.

Nothing is more helpless than a naked man dying on a cross. God's greatest work was done on a cross. All Jesus has and gives is a cross. The church was born, and still lives, on a cross. The cross appalls, compels, and then slays. There is no sinner for whom Jesus did not die. Everyone needs to know that. There is no sin the cross cannot take away. The cross is not a freak experience. It is a universal truth incarnated. Jesus was not on the cross for merely six hours. In a sense, He was there for thirty-three years. Jesus is the source of salvation; the cross was the means. God's power is made perfect in weakness (2 Corinthians 12:6–10). Although crucified through weakness, Jesus lives by the power of God (2 Corinthians 13:4). Therefore, the gospel can only be received by the weak, not the strong. No man can stand at the cross and boast.

CHRIST, THE WISDOM OF GOD

The greatest power of God lies in His wisdom. Christianity is only authentic with the cross at its center. Man thinks the cross is grotesque; God made it into His glory. The German philosopher and atheist Friedrich Nietzsche idolized power. He despised Jesus because he thought He was weak. Nietzsche is dead; the gospel is still preached. Christ crucified is the embodiment of the wisdom of God. What a God! The sin that underlies all sin is presumption (Psalm 19:13; 2 Peter 2:10). Man presumes that the way he thinks is the way God thinks, or should think. Psychology promises to make life *better*. Christ gives sinners life, *period*! Dead men need life, not rehabilitation (Ephesians 2). Man wants salvation from war, poverty, and disease. Christ on the cross saves us from sin. Man cannot solve war, poverty, or disease until he is saved from sin. Sin can be cured only at the cross.

To the intellectually proud, the cross is still folly. Man wants power, not wisdom—enlightenment, not faith. Man has taken the cross away from Jesus; some would take it away from the church. One cannot hold to the cross and at the same time hold to hatred and sin. The power of God has always been to raise the dead. At the cross God raises sinners from the dead.

At the cross Jesus died to save a world that did not want to be saved. What a Savior! Paul determined to know nothing save Christ and Him crucified (1 Corinthians 2:1–5). Believe it! Teach it! Never lose faith in the power of the gospel! Quit trying to be godly without God, Christian without Christ, spiritual without the Spirit. Do not "try" to live the Christian life—live life as a Christian.

Six Miracles at Calvary

Matthew 27:45–54; Mark 15:33–39; Luke 23:44–47

"And behold, the veil of the temple was torn in two from top to bottom; and the earth shook and the rocks were split. The tombs were opened, and many bodies of the saints who had fallen asleep were raised" (Matthew 27:51, 52).

God warned the Jews time and time again. There was no excuse for the Jews not to become believers. Jewish leaders knew that Jesus was divine; but, in their hate and blindness, they killed Him anyway. Even Pilate knew who He was (Matthew 27:18).

Look at the miracles that took place before the crucifixion. During the arrest in the garden, when Jesus said, "I am He," many in the mob drew back and fell on the ground (John 18:6). Awesome! This should have stopped the whole sordid affair!

Then there was the miracle with Malchus' ear! Do not be too harsh with Peter. He was willing to fight and die for Jesus. He knew how to use that sword, and upon whom he could use it (a slave). What statement was Peter making by doing this action? "Yes, we are outnumbered, and we will lose—but some of you will die." He flicked off Malchus' ear, but Jesus healed it. This was the last miracle for the Jews before Jesus went to the cross. Jesus could manage anything!

We must not forget the miracle that never happened! Read and reread Matthew 26:50–56; Mark 14:46–50; Luke 22:50, 51; John 18:10–14. Jesus told Peter He could have called twelve legions of angels (Matthew 26:53, 54) . . . but He did not!

1. DARKNESS

Those who will not believe, if they are given time, cannot believe. Why have we neglected and overlooked the miracles? Jesus was on the cross six hours. The first three belonged to the crowd; the last three belonged to God! The darkness was a preview of hell (Matthew 8:12; 2 Peter 2:4; Jude 6, 13). It is Christ or hell!

This darkness was not an eclipse of the sun. An eclipse lasts only a few minutes and cannot happen during a full moon. Passover came during a full moon. The darkness was eerie with quietness, except for the cries of three dying men with dropping blood (Matthew 27:45; Mark 15:33; Luke 23:44). The shame of Calvary smothered the sun. Those present could see only darkness and hear only silence.

2. THE VEIL

At 3:00 p.m. the priests were on duty at the temple. Jesus cried with a loud voice. Before their startled eyes, the veil separating the Holy Place from the Holy of Holies was torn from top to bottom (Matthew 27:51; Mark 15:38; Luke 23:45). God was gone from an earthly location. The law of Moses was gone; the Levitical priesthood was gone. No wonder many priests obeyed the gospel (Acts 6:7).

3. THE EARTHQUAKE

The suspense was surely terrifying. No wonder even Roman soldiers were awed at the earthquake (Matthew 27:51, 54). Rocks, some of the hardest substances on earth, were split. Everything shook except the cross!

4. THE OPENED GRAVES

The Jews had demanded of Jesus a sign. God gave them six miracles at Calvary. The splitting of the rocks was brute force; the opening of the graves was brilliant design (Matthew 27:52, 53). What an unusual earthquake! Only selected graves were opened! No wonder the spectators beat their breasts (Luke 23:48). God was still teaching, warning, and reaching out to the Jews. This also proves that the events on the Day of Pentecost (the beginning of the church in Acts 2) were no accident. Peter began the first gospel sermon, testifying, ". . . as you yourselves know" (Acts 2:22). God had given them fifty days to think about the cross. Peter gave them the solution—Christ.

5. THE GRAVE CLOTHES

John outran Peter, yet he stopped. He found only an empty tomb. When he followed Peter into the tomb, he saw evidence of a resurrected Savior (John 20:1–9; Luke 24:1–12). The last thing the enemies wanted was an empty tomb. The disciples would have clothed Jesus; they would not have disrobed Him. Enemies would not have taken the time to disrobe Him. Grave clothes were enough evidence for John. He was the first to believe! We, too, must think logically about this!

6. THE RESURRECTED SAINTS

The graves were opened on Friday (Matthew 27:50–53). The resurrected saints did not walk until Sunday. To remain ceremonially clean, the Jews could not greet their loved ones. Uncle John! Aunt Ruth! What a monumental miracle! What would you have done if you had been there?

The cross . . .
there is no other way!

QUESTIONS FOR STUDY AND DISCUSSION

1. Review the oxymorons given in the "More Confusing Than Amusing" section of this chapter. Give other examples. How have you experienced these in your life?
2. Discuss the statement "God does heart transplants." Give biblical and/or personal examples of radical change affected by Christianity.
3. Who was in control at the cross? How do the Scriptures make this clear?
4. What was the last miracle Jesus performed for the Jews? Describe it.
5. Name the six miracles at the time of Jesus' death. What was the significance of each one? Which do you find particularly intriguing?

8

"MORE CONFUSING THAN AMUSING"

PROPHECY

"God forbid that I should glory, save in the cross of our Lord Jesus Christ." Those who believe that miracles and prophecies have ceased may have little interest in prophecy. *Think about it!* Prophecy is our powerful tool. There are 30,000 promises in the Bible.[1] God kept every one of His promises. Floyd Hamilton noted that there are 332 fulfilled prophecies concerning Jesus in the Old Testament.[2] Some are very specific. No other religion has a prophesied founder and Savior!

Gene Greer[3] said that Jesus claimed authority 9 times, claimed to be the Son of God 90 times, claimed to be sent by God 33 times, and claimed to be the Messiah 31 times! It is not by chance that Jesus began His public ministry claiming to be the prophesied Messiah (Isaiah 61:1–3; Luke 4:16–27). The listeners did not misunderstand. In anger they tried to kill Him (Luke 4:28–30). Men tried to abort His ministry in His own hometown!

Consider the many prophecies Jesus fulfilled.[4] He

---

[1]Herbert Lockyer, *All the Promises of the Bible* (Grand Rapids, Mich.: Zondervan, 1962), 10.

[2]Floyd Hamilton, *The Basis of Christian Faith*, rev. and enl. (New York: Harper and Row, 1964), 160.

[3]Gene Greer, preacher in Heidenhammer, Texas. Conversation by telephone, n.d.

[4]See Hugo McCord, "Jesus: The Fulfillment of Prophecy in His Life," in "Jesus Christ, the Divine Son of God," *Truth for Today* (May 2000): 9–17.

was the seed of Abraham (Genesis 22:18; Romans 4:13–25; Acts 7:1–6; Galatians 3:6–16), a prophet like Moses (Deuteronomy 18:15–22; Acts 3:22–26), and the seed of David (John 7:42; Romans 1:3; 2 Timothy 2:8). He spoke in parables (Psalm 78:2; Matthew 13:34, 35). He was the son of a virgin (Isaiah 7:14; Matthew 1:23–25), a Galilean (Isaiah 9:1, 2; Mark 14:70; Luke 22:59), the light of the Gentiles (Isaiah 49:6; Acts 13:46, 47), a lowly king (Zechariah 9:9; Matthew 21:1–8), and the Branch (Jeremiah 23:5; Hebrews 7:14). Having been called out of Egypt (Hosea 11:1; Matthew 2:15), He became a Nazarene (Matthew 2:23). Jesus was declared before the foundation of the world (Ephesians 1:3, 4; 3:9–11; 1 Peter 1:20). The "slain Lamb" is the center of all history.

Some of these prophecies are given in generalities. However, especially in regard to the cross, there are some minute specifics: the manner of death (Psalm 22:16; Zechariah 12:10; John 12:32), a public death (Deuteronomy 21:22, 23; Acts 5:30; 10:39; 13:29; Galatians 3:13; 1 Peter 2:24), betrayal by a friend (Psalm 41:9; Matthew 26:14, 15; 27:3–10) for thirty pieces of silver (Zechariah 11:12; Matthew 26:14, 15; 27:3–10), silence before accusers (Psalm 38:13; Isaiah 53:7; Matthew 26:59–63; Mark 14:55–61; 1 Peter 2:23, 24), being with thieves (Isaiah 53:12; Matthew 27:38; Mark 15:28; Luke 23:39–43), having pierced hands and feet (Psalm 22:16; Zechariah 12:10; John 20:27), the casting of lots for clothes (Psalm 22:18; Mark 15:24; John 19:23, 24), having no bones broken (Psalm 34:20; John 19:36), being offered gall and vinegar to drink (Psalm 69:21; Matthew 27:34; John 19:28–30), the exclamation (Psalm 22:1; Matthew 27:46), being buried with the rich (Isaiah 53:9; Matthew 27:57–60), and becoming the rejected cornerstone (Psalm 118:22, 23; Matthew 21:42; Acts 4:11; Romans

9:32, 33). The lowly king who came riding upon a donkey (Zechariah 9:9; Matthew 21:1–11) was declared by Peter on Pentecost as "both Lord and Christ" (Acts 2:36).

Isaiah is called the "Messianic Prophet." Isaiah 53 is the "Holy of Holies" in the Old Testament, the "Suffering Servant Song." Six hundred years before Christ, Isaiah was inspired by God to give a detailed picture of the Messiah. The Book of Isaiah is quoted more than fifty times in the New Testament.[5] The Jews never understood Isaiah 53. They wanted a political military victory. The idea of a suffering, dead Savior never crossed their minds. Be merciful. It is difficult to imagine the God of heaven dying upon a cross! It is one thing to believe Jesus is God; it is another thing to believe God is Jesus!

Phrases from Isaiah 53 are repeated at least six times in the New Testament![6] Amazing grace! The One dying on the cross was the same One who created the world! God cannot countenance sin—not even in His Son, who was made to be sin. Philip told the Ethiopian nobleman that this man was Jesus (Acts 8:30–35).

All the verbs in Isaiah 53 are in the past tense. The future is declared as history. God (Jesus) is the same yesterday, today, and forever. With God the past, present, and future are all the same in reality. God's prophecies are so true that they are past. Jesus fulfilled all prophecy. He prophesied His own death, burial, and resurrection.[7] The life of Christ is the most certified fact on earth!

---

[5]Gleason L. Archer and Gregory Chirichigno, *Old Testament Quotations in the New Testament* (Chicago: Moody Press, 1983), 92–134.

[6]Ibid., 120–24.

[7]See Matthew 16:21 (and Mark 8:31; Luke 9:22); 17:22, 23 (and Mark 9:30–32; Luke 9:43, 44); 20:17–19 (and Mark 10:32–34; Luke 18:31–33); Luke 24:7, 44–46; John 13:19.

The Big Words of the Cross, 1

Romans 5:11–21

"For if by the transgression of the one, death reigned through the one, much more those who receive the abundance of grace and of the gift of righteousness will reign in life through the One, Jesus Christ" (Romans 5:17).

Atonement! Without holiness, no man can see God (Hebrews 12:14). Sin violates and eliminates holiness. In sin man separated himself from a holy God. No sin can enter heaven. No sinner has the right or the reason to stand in the presence of a holy God. Every sin and every sinner will be punished—either at the cross or in hell. Can man in sin be saved? If so, how, when, and by whom? Sin is the greatest of all problems, but Jesus died to solve it. Sinners do not merely need to be saved—they need a Savior!

John the Baptist was privileged to announce, "Behold, the Lamb of God who takes away the sin of the world!" (John 1:29, 36). Jesus did not come to seek the saved but to seek the lost (Luke 19:10). Calvary is the incredible revelation of a pardoning God. The atonement is God's own mystery!

Obviously, atonement is beyond our comprehension, beyond our compensation. Faith believes that which can never be understood. Atonement is not a story for our intellect, but a sanctuary for our faith.

Nothing in all of history is more amazing than the

influence of Jesus. God invites us to plumb the depths of the cross. We must be stunned into silence and overwhelmed by gratitude. Atonement is the centerpiece in the Bible—it is what separates Christianity from all other religions. One day in time—at the cross—sinful man saw the eternal love of God (John 3:16).

It is better to accept a theology we cannot fully understand than to buy clarity at the price of inadequacy. Sin has to be atoned. There cannot be "at-one-ment" with God without atonement. Jesus suffered the penalty that sin deserved. Christianity depends on the crucifixion. If sinners could have been saved another way, then God would have been a fiend to sacrifice His only Son. The accusers unknowingly spoke a profound truth: "He saved others; He cannot save Himself" (Mark 15:31; see Luke 23:35). Jesus has no peers and no rivals. He is the Lion of Judah (Revelation 5:5), but He is also the Lamb. We identify more easily with the Lion. Victory came not by the Lion, but by the Lamb (1 Peter 1:18, 19). The great teaching about the Lamb is in Revelation.[8] The saved are listed in the Lamb's book of life (Philippians 4:3; Revelation 3:5; 17:8; 20:12, 15; 22:19). Judgment begins with those listed in that book (1 Peter 4:17). Others are condemned already (John 3:16–18).

Atonement makes amends, makes things right, gives satisfaction to a wronged person. Atonement demonstrates that "God is right." God is right about our problem—sin. He is right about the solution—the cross. Atonement is like a diamond: You cannot see it all from any one direction. Cardinal errors result from emphasizing

---

[8]See Revelation 5:6, 12, 13; 6:16; 7:9, 10, 14; 12:11; 13:8; 14:1, 4; 21:9; 22:1, 3.

some facets over others. This is admiration, not adoration. Jesus died on a cross—that is history. Jesus died for me—that is salvation. We must learn to believe, accept, and love that which we cannot fully understand.

"JUST," "JUSTICE," AND "JUSTIFICATION"

It has been said that Romans is the heart of the Scriptures and Romans 3:20–26 is the heart of Romans: ". . . that He would be just and the justifier." Atonement is built upon justice. The Bible uses "justification" and "righteousness" in basically the same way. Obviously, one cannot preach justification without justice. How can God justify the guilty? Time and forgetfulness do not cancel sin. Sin cannot be fixed. Even God does not fix sin. The sin penalty must be paid; sin must be punished. Jesus paid it all! God's answer to sin is the cross.

Culture stumbles over this (1 Corinthians 1:22–25). Man cannot see himself lost in sin. Universalism says, "God is too good to allow you to go to hell. You are too good to go to hell"—but "good enough" never is! There is no justice without punishment. A holy God cannot allow sin to remain unpunished. God is *just*. Do not accept this "God is loving and will overlook sin" idea! Mercy cannot cheat justice. God cannot be less than God. This concept must be understood. To fail here is to fail everywhere. Justice is a higher principle than sentimental love. What justice demanded, grace provided. Since sinners cannot save themselves, a Savior is demanded. Jesus is the Savior. What man could not do, God did in man (Jesus).

Justice is the heart of biblical theology. Understand justice! To believe in the cross is to accept justice and to accept hell. Love cannot make sense apart from justice (holiness). Without justice, grace is unnecessary. Without justice, the cross is insanity. Love cannot make sense apart from holiness. God is a God of justice. Unless guilt matters, the whole world is meaningless. Sin must be justified—not overlooked (1 Corinthians 6:11).

The incarnation of Jesus could not save us. The perfect life of Christ could not save us. The perfect teachings of Jesus, by themselves, could not save us. There must be blood: ". . . and without shedding of blood there is no forgiveness" (Hebrews 9:22). There must be death: ". . . since a death has taken place" (Hebrews 9:15–17; see 2:9; Romans 5:10; Colossians 1:22).

It was not love that nailed Jesus to the cross—it was justice. God is *just*. He also is the *justifier*. God is *right*. God provided by grace what man could not do by works. This is why Jesus cried out, "It is finished!" when He died upon the cross. "He paid a debt He did not owe; I owed a debt I could not pay."[9] Jesus could save Himself or save us. He gave Himself to save us. The Judge of man became the Savior of man (John 5:22–27).

Therefore, salvation begins and ends with justification. We have been justified. "Just-as-if-I'd [never sinned]" sounds better than it actually is. We have sinned. The justice of God is so contrary to us that it even takes Christians by surprise! Still, God cannot save us until we let Him! Our only motivation is the cross of Christ. Justice is the heart of the Christian faith.

"SUBSTITUTION"
The middle cross at Calvary did not belong to Jesus; it belonged to me! His crucifixion was *vicarious, represen-*

---

[9]Author unknown, "He Paid a Debt," *Songs of Faith and Praise*, comp. and ed. Alton H. Howard (West Monroe, La.: Howard Publishing Co., 1994).

tative, and *substitutionary*! The foundation of atonement is substitution. Christ took a death that belongs to us; we take a life that belongs to Him. Without substitution, the cross is only a story about a brave man who died on a cross. Since we cannot save ourselves, someone else must. What did I contribute to my salvation? My sin! Jesus is a perfect substitute in everything we were meant to be. The Son of God became the Son of Man, so that the sons of men might become sons of God. Christ's blood was first given for us and then given to us.

Can a person benefit from another's suffering and sacrifice? Yes! Life itself is filled with the concept of substitution. It is logical, lawful, and expedient. The sacrificial system of the Old Testament teaches us this profound truth. The "scapegoat" is the viable example. Glorious Isaiah 53 reveals the depth of substitution. The Bible affirms substitution.[10] Jesus was made to be sin. Never was there more injustice and justice than at the cross! There cannot be salvation from sin without a living Savior. How can the unrighteous be righteous? Think! Our righteousness is a "declared righteousness" (see Romans 3:25, 26; KJV; Philippians 3:9; James 2:23). No one can declare himself righteous (Romans 3:9, 10, 20). Self-justification is impossible. It is God who justifies (Romans 8:33), and He does this freely (Romans 3:24). This is a gift. A gift must have *both* a giver and a receiver. A gift is not a gift until it is received. Further, a gift is not a gift until it is used. We have a sin problem. Jesus as our substitute is the only solution.

God cannot overlook or dismiss sin. He assumed our

---

[10]See Romans 5:5–10; Ephesians 1:3–13; Philippians 3:7–10; Hebrews 2:9, 14–17; 7:25; 9:28; 10:10; 12:1, 2; 1 Peter 2:24; 1 John 2:1, 2.

sin and sentenced Himself for it. God's holiness was honored. Our sin has been punished, and we have been redeemed. God declares sinners righteous. This is a legal (lawful) declaration. It is "justified justification."

God is not making bad people good or evil people holy. Christians are faithful—not perfect. We are tempted and sinful; we fall short (Romans 3:9–12). Christians still live on earth, in time, and in the flesh. Paul said that nothing good dwells in the flesh (Romans 7:18). Christians are at war . . . with Satan, sin, and self. However, Christians who are walking in the Light are constantly cleansed (1 John 1:7). God pronounces Christians legally righteous, free from any liability to the broken law, because He Himself, in His Son, bore the penalty. We are baptized into Christ and put on Christ in this act (Romans 6:3, 4; Galatians 3:26, 27). To be "declared righteous" changes not only our status, but also our character and our conduct.

There cannot be justification without atonement. Faith receives what grace freely offers. The cross is God's impenetrable mystery, a love greater than our minds can fathom. God is not, in reality, Someone we can understand, but He is Someone we can trust.

Critics of Christianity abhor substitution. Substitution magnifies sacrifice. The entire concept of biblical religion is based on sacrifice. From Genesis to Revelation, God ordained sacrifice. Jesus cannot be reduced to a good teacher, a benefactor, or a mere person—He is our sacrifice. God is both the reconciler and the reconciled. Jesus is humanity's substitute. Jesus did not offer an animal; He offered Himself. Hebrews reveals Jesus as the unique priest and sacrifice. We read, "Christ saves us as a priest, by offering Himself as a sacrifice for our sins."[11] In the Old Testament, God had to see the blood before He saved the family as Israel was leaving Egypt (Exodus 12:13). Everyone rescued by God has thereby been purchased for God. Our bodies belong to God three times over—by creation, by redemption, and by the indwelling of the Holy Spirit (1 Corinthians 6:19, 20). The heart of Isaiah 53 is sacrifice. Jesus is the Lamb slain from the foundation of the world (Revelation 13:8).

"ADOPTION"

Nothing in ministry is as exciting as helping parents adopt a child. In closure, we all think, "This child does not grasp how blessed he is." This is a neglected facet of Christianity. We seldom talk about or study adoption. Why? It involves the Holy Spirit. Are we more afraid of the Holy Spirit than of Satan? We are born again of water and the Spirit (John 3:3–7). Being led by the Spirit, we become sons of God. He is the Spirit of adoption. He bears witness with our spirit (Romans 8:14–18). This makes us "fellow heirs with Christ." God wants sons, not slaves. Christians are sons—not just freed slaves. God, who remained at a distance in the Old Testament, is now "Abba! Father!" This is beyond our understanding! Redemption makes adoption possible. The Holy Spirit cries, "Abba! Father!" in our hearts (Galatians 4:4–7). Jesus lives in our hearts by the Holy Spirit.

Amazing grace! By grace God predestined us for adoption by Jesus. We are accepted by God in the Beloved. Redemption is through His blood. Upon obeying the gospel of salvation, we were sealed with the Holy

---

[11]Charles Hodge, *Systematic Theology,* vol. 2 (New York: Scribner, Armstrong, and Co., 1876), 555.

Spirit of promise (Ephesians 1:3–14). This is a "crown jewel" in the Scriptures. Here is the basis of our faith. John revealed the grand love of God—that we forgiven sinners could be called the sons of God. Now we are sons! (1 John 3:1, 2). What a profound thought! Privilege! In this we see the Roman concept of freedom and then sonship. Free! Restored! Adopted! To claim Christ is to claim acquittal. Calvary is the incredible revelation of a pardoning God! We are incapable of winning the battle alone. God does what we cannot do, so we can be what we dare not think.

The cross . . .
there is no other way!

QUESTIONS FOR STUDY AND DISCUSSION

1. Discuss a few of the Old Testament prophecies which were fulfilled by the life and death of Jesus. Which ones have the greatest impact on your faith in Him as the Messiah?

2. How were various phrases in Isaiah 53 fulfilled in Christ?

3. Study the dictionary definitions of "atonement" and "justification." What do these two words say about what Christ has done for us?

4. Consider the images of the Lion and the Lamb. How does each describe Jesus?

5. Explore the concept of "substitution." Read Romans 5; Ephesians 1; Philippians 3; Hebrews 2:9–17; 7:25; 9:28; 10:10; 12:1, 2; 1 Peter 2:24; 1 John 2:1, 2.

6. Discuss the statement "Jesus was made to be sin—not a sinner." Why was this necessary for our salvation?

9

"MORE CONFUSING THAN AMUSING"

SIN

"God forbid that I should glory, save in the cross of our Lord Jesus Christ." What is the most consistently avoided, shunned, and rejected word? *"Sin"*! Even in the church! Culture has banished the word "sin." Sinners are no longer called "sinners." Psychology does not even use the word "sin." This is why it fails to help people deal with guilt. Our culture has turned theology into psychology, the cross into a couch, the church into a rehabilitation program, worship into therapy, and damnation into dysfunction.

The church lives to convert the world—not to be swallowed by it. How can you help someone to be saved if he does not know he is lost? How can believers pretend sin does not exist? Man's only problem is sin.

The only topic in the Bible is sin. God gave the law of Moses to make people aware of sin (Romans 3:20). Sin cannot be fixed; it can only be forgiven. The Jew was right when he asked, "Who can forgive sins but God alone?" (Mark 2:7; Luke 5:21). With mankind, the problem of sin is insurmountable! It is not why God finds it difficult to forgive, but why He finds it necessary to do so at all! Can man in sin be saved? Every sin and every sinner will be punished! God is "holy" and far removed from sin (Isaiah 6:3; see Revelation 4:8). He is transcendent holiness. A holy God cannot touch sin.

COSMIC CONSEQUENCES

"Just one bite of fruit?" That is all it took! No murder, immorality, theft, abuse, or ill treatment was required to coerce mankind to sin. Everything changed in heaven, in hell, and on earth when Adam and Eve sinned! All was different with God, man, and Satan! Everything within man changed. He became alienated eternally from God and distanced from his mate. Mankind would never be the same. No wonder God said, "Where are you?" (Genesis 3:9). Read Genesis 2 and 3 and tremble! Man is a fallen, damned sinner. Anything man, as a sinner, can be is an insult to God Almighty.

There is more to this history than "one bite." Adam and Eve allowed Satan to enter their lives. They listened to Satan, believed Satan, and obeyed Satan. They disobeyed God. God is God, and man is not. Man is offended to think that God has a claim over him.

A person can only be tempted when he is led away by his own lusts (James 1). He sins within before he sins without. Sin is the supreme choice of self. Sin is the refusal to let God be God; it is man trying to be more than man. Sin is thinking man knows more, or knows better, than God. Man's relationship with God is now broken, betrayed, and destroyed. Sin matters to God. Sin is cosmic treason. Tragically, man decided to become his own god.

Sinners are now dead in their sins (Ephesians 2). The wages of sin is death (Romans 6:23). Our sins eternally alienate us from God (Isaiah 59:2, 3). All the war, violence, and chaos in history began with that "one bite." God told Adam about this before it ever happened. However, God was displaced. Since then, Satan has been the god, prince, and father of the world (John 8:44; 12:31; 14:30; 16:11; 2 Corinthians 4:4).

To be saved, sinners must see sin as God sees it. Revival cannot come until sinners sense the horror of sin. People who do not fear God do not fear sin. People with a holy view of God sense the enormity of sin.

God hates sin, and we must hate sin, but, tragically, too many do not hate sin as sin. The more holy we become, the more we hate sin because of what it does to our relationship with God. God is right. Our problem is sin; the solution is the cross. Without sin, the cross would have been unnecessary.

HOPELESS, HELPLESS, AND HAPLESS

Man in sin cannot save himself. He cannot earn, buy, or deserve salvation. He cannot know enough or do enough to be saved. Since man cannot save himself, someone else must. This means that we are saved by God's grace, not by human merit. All that a sinner can do is repent. No one can do that for him.

Jesus did not come to die for hurts or habits. He died for our sins (Romans 5:6, 8; 1 Peter 1:18, 19). We are washed in His blood (1 Corinthians 6:11; Hebrews 10:19; Revelation 1:5; 7:14). Jesus was made to be *sin,* but not a *sinner* (2 Corinthians 5:14–21). The choice is ours. We can have our sins punished at the cross through Jesus or have the punishment upon us in hell.

Jesus died to save a world that did not want to be saved. He forgave sins that few wished to have forgiven.

Jesus died on a cross—that is history. Jesus died for me—that is salvation. The only way I can deal with sin is to die to it (Romans 6).

The Big Words of the Cross, 2

2 Corinthians 5:17–21

"... *God was in Christ reconciling the world to Himself, not counting their trespasses against them, and He has committed to us the word of reconciliation"* (2 Corinthians 5:19).

"RECONCILIATION"

Salvation was and is by substitution. The object is reconciliation. Discard all you think you know concerning forgiveness and reconciliation. Start over as we walk through this process. Get this right. Forgiveness is "in" today. Children are taught to say "I'm sorry" without thought, depth, repentance, or regret. Apology is "in"; confession of responsibility is "out." The Scriptures teach profound repentance. The word "apologize" is not found in the Scriptures.

Picture two people who are close friends, and then the relationship is violated and broken. To reconcile them is to restore the relationship to the way it was. With reconciliation, the lost is found; the dead is made alive; the sinful is forgiven. How can this be? First, the offended must want this restoration more than anything else. Second, the offender must want this restoration more than anything else. Society, today, just wants to be free from responsibility. *Both* the offended and the offender must be willing to pay any price for restoration. This is crucial!

Forgiveness does not mean ending an argument yet living apart. Reconciliation is not a "Cold War." Society only wants freedom without accountability. There is no reconciliation without satisfaction.

The offender is at the mercy of the offended. Our text tells us that God reconciled us to Himself in Christ. God reconciled the world to Himself; God did not reconcile Himself to the world. Who moves first? God does! Reconciliation is not a business transaction. Jesus died for me before I repented! God provided forgiveness for me (with the gospel) before I was born! God wants sinners back! Sinners must want to be taken back. Man is eternally lost unless God acts. We are His enemies, but we can be reconciled! Who moves first? Love moves first!

- Forgiveness is impossible without the grace of the offended.
- Forgiveness is impossible without the repentance of the offender.

It only takes *one* to forgive. It takes *two* to reconcile. You cannot help a man who will not help himself. Forgiveness is an unnatural act. The offended does not wish to pay the price; the offender does not want to repent. Nevertheless, they must do *both* to reconcile. Without reconciliation, forgiveness fails.

Forgiveness is not the end (as our society thinks); rather, forgiveness is the means, and reconciliation is the end. Forgiveness does not merely free us from penalty; forgiveness allows us to restore a broken relationship.

LAWS OF "FORGIVENESS"

Shakespeare said, "To be, or not to be, that is the

question."[1] Scripture says, "To forgive, or not to forgive—that is the issue." I must forgive. I must be forgiven. That is life. Forgiveness is the bridge over which all must walk. What do we do when we forgive? What do we do when we accept forgiveness? "Be kind to one another, tenderhearted, forgiving each other, just as God in Christ also has forgiven you" (Ephesians 4:32). Forgiveness begins with kindness. Be kind first! Then practice the laws of forgiveness.

(1) The unforgiving cannot be forgiven. (Read Jesus' prayer in Matthew 6:12–15; Mark 11:24–26; Luke 11:4; see also Matthew 18:35; 2 Corinthians 2:7; Luke 6:37.) Do not just learn the theory—start the practice! Our paramount purpose must be to learn to forgive. The offender is totally helpless before the offended. To end that, be the first to forgive!

(2) The offended must forgive, if only for sanity's sake! Without forgiveness, one can become bitter, mean, and angry. The past must not rule the future. Without forgiveness, one lives in chains. If you wait until the offender repents, you can waste your life waiting. Once you forgive in your heart, it ceases to be a primary issue—whether or not the offender repents. The chair and the plate belonging to the prodigal son were there even when he was in the far country (Luke 15), but he had to repent and return to use them. The prodigal left home to sin; to be forgiven, he had to stop sinning and return home (Luke 15:11–24). You cannot have forgiveness while living in the far country and sinning. The forgiveness was there—the unmerited yet conditional forgiveness of God. The father could not force the prodigal to return.

---

[1]William Shakespeare *Hamlet* 3.1.56.

God cannot save us until we let Him.

(3) There cannot be forgiveness without repentance. The innocent do not need forgiveness; they need to be defended and vindicated. Sinners are not innocent. Sinners are not victims. We must accept full responsibility for our sin. "I did it." Then we must repent (change). Someone may say, "It doesn't matter." Things that do not matter do not need forgiveness. Sin, hurt, offense, and betrayal matter! Sinners are violators! When we are violated, then we rebuke; when there is repentance, we forgive (Luke 17:3, 4).

Sin matters. It must be dealt with. Do not be too hard on Peter. He was willing to forgive seven times (Matthew 18:21–35). Jesus multiplied that seventy times! Jesus Himself used the "seven" in Luke 17:3, 4. Peter was listening; but he was not thinking, learning, or practicing. Nothing is too big or too much to forgive (Matthew 18:21–35). At the same time, forgiveness is not license to sin (Galatians 6:7).

God did not say "I forgive you" to Adam and Eve. They were driven out of the Garden of Eden. Jesus did not yell "I forgive you" from the cross, although He did ask God to remit the sin of those who crucified Him (Luke 23:34).

Reconciliation is more than forgiveness. To reduce salvation to forgiveness only is heresy. Repentance is not just turning from sin, but also turning to God. The prodigal could have been forgiven yet made a slave. God wants sons, not slaves (Luke 15). Sinners cannot accomplish their reconciliation, but they can reject it. The popular attitude "I am not here to judge you" is foolish! Repentance can never be too soon, but it can be too late.

(4) Forgiveness does not guarantee a painless future. Forgiven sin still has consequences. Time and forgetfulness are not forgiveness. God remembers our sins no more (Jeremiah 31:34; Hebrews 8:12; 10:17), but this is not "spiritual amnesia." Sin has consequences. King David's baby died. Forgiven Israel was punished. Jerusalem was "wiped out like a dish" (A.D. 70). Sinners still have nightmares. "My sin is ever before me" (Psalm 51:3b).

Forgiveness is the most costly thing on earth (Romans 5:10). Forgiving is not forgetting; it is starting all over again. Forgiveness is a gift. Only when we grasp our forgiveness do we love (Luke 7:36–50). Gifts are to be humbly received and greatly enjoyed.

"PROPITIATION"

The word "propitiation" is one we cannot spell; we even mispronounce it. This word is a difficult concept because it was a heathen practice. Pagan idols were portrayed as having childish whims that had to be appeased. God does not have moods; He is above hurt feelings. In Jesus' time "propitiation" referred to appeasing the anger of an idol by making a blood sacrifice. God did not appease Himself. He created a salvation by which He was justified. God Himself justified Himself. Jesus provided this propitiation Himself, by Himself. In a sense, God bore our punishment! Expiation (making atonement) makes propitiation (reconciliation) possible. The propitiation is the expiation.

Man must be righteous, but he cannot create righteousness. It is of God, but He cannot confer it on sinners. Sinners cannot pay back, bribe, or impress God with lavish gifts. Jesus is the final, perfect sacrifice. He took upon

Himself first our flesh, then our sin. Jesus is *both* our High Priest and our sacrifice (Hebrews 2:14–18). He is *both* our Lord and Savior (Acts 2:36). He must be our Lord to be our Savior. Jesus is our vicarious sacrifice—the heart of Jewish sacrifices. He was not made guilty; He was made to be sin as a substitute (2 Corinthians 5:17–21). Propitiation enforces the enormity of sin. Love without wrath is sentimentality. You will never understand the cross until you realize that God put Jesus to death. If you can think of living without God, then focus on Jesus at the cross. Divine grace satisfied divine wrath by a divine self-sacrifice. Too many sinners want forgiveness without reconciliation. They wish to be free from responsibility but not to be restored. To be forgiven means we can get along together again.

"EXPIATION"

Only Christianity says it is impossible for sinners to save themselves. Only Christianity offers a Savior, Jesus (Acts 2:36). Propitiation and expiation are so intertwined that it is difficult to separate them. Expiation is the divine side; propitiation is the application. You expiate a sin; you propitiate a person. Expiation is doctrinal; propitiation is personal. Expiation is the removal of guilt; propitiation is the removal of wrath. Jesus is our "mercy seat" (Romans 3:25, 26). Our righteousness is a faith-righteousness in Christ. The blood is our expiatory sacrifice. This is the heart of the heart of the heart of our faith. The cross is where the sin of man is judged. To expiate is to pay the penalty, the price (1 John 2:1, 2). We were bought with a price. Sinners are not declared innocent, but they are considered "not guilty" (Hebrews 2:17, 18; 1 John 4:9–11; 1 Peter 2:9, 10). Jesus is our "Passover" (1 Corinthians 5:7). He covered our sins, allowing God to put them behind His back (Romans 8:1, 2; see Isaiah 38:17).

God did not stand apart from the cross in petulant anger. He involved Himself in our plight. In Christ, He took the penalty of our sins upon Himself—not in mechanical substitution, but in profoundly personal love. God cannot and will not forgive and accept us except at the cross.

"IMPUTATION"

The idea of imputed righteousness is profound yet simple. Sinful man cannot be righteous; therefore, imputed righteousness is the only kind of righteousness he can have. Justification has been called "the supreme paradox of the gospel." God accepts sinners as being just (Romans 8:1, 2).

Imputation is an accounting term. Another's riches are placed in my account. Our sins were imputed to Christ, and His righteousness is imputed to us (Isaiah 53:5, 6, 10, 11; 1 Peter 2:24; Romans 4:11; 14:9). Read and reread Philippians 3:7–11. Tragically, we would prefer to merit grace, but grace cannot be merited! Burton Coffman well said, "Nothing that man could ever do in a million years of righteous living could ever earn the tiniest fraction of the salvation God gives to men in Christ."[2] Imputed righteousness eliminates human pride.

"RANSOM"

The best known and most misunderstood facet of

---

[2]James Burton Coffman, *Commentary on Romans* (Austin, Tex.: Firm Foundation Publishing House, 1973), 122.

atonement is "ransom." God does not negotiate with anyone! He did not buy sinners back from Satan. We are "sold under sin" (Romans 7:14; NKJV), but not to Satan. God, not Satan, was satisfied at the cross (1 John 2:1, 2). Satan is the "accuser" (Revelation 12:9, 10). How could God be holy while allowing sin? Sin has to be paid for. Man cannot sin without consequence. A ransom is the purchase price for freeing slaves, and sinners are servants of sin. God silenced Satan at the cross forever (Matthew 20:28; Galatians 3:13; 1 Timothy 2:5, 6; Titus 2:14, 15). We are redeemed by the blood of the Lamb. What Satan thought was his greatest victory was his final defeat! Our sins will either be paid for at the cross, or they will be paid for in hell. We make the choice. Jesus died for us—for our sin and for our death. He did not die as a martyr for a cause, but freely gave His life as a ransom. Jesus made sin forgivable and man savable. Our Redeemer lives!

To whom was this ransom paid? Not to society. Society has no law or court to deal with sin. The ransom was paid in order to satisfy justice, holiness. We were bought with a tremendous price. Upon being ransomed, the debtor is totally owned. A ransom is satisfaction for the insult of sin. The penalty of law (Romans 6:23) is paid, and its sanctity is vindicated. The ransom reveals the seriousness, sheer depth, and horror of sin. Salvation is ours when we believe and obey. Jesus not only dethroned Satan, but He also dealt with sin. In overcoming sin, Jesus overcame death. The sin-debt is unpayable except by the miracle of grace. The redeemed must never forget!

The cross . . .
there is no other way!

QUESTIONS FOR STUDY AND DISCUSSION

1. What is society's view of sin and personal responsibility?
2. Discuss the various definitions of sin proposed by the author: (a) the supreme choice of self, (b) thinking that one knows better than God, (c) cosmic treason, (d) man's decision to become his own God. Give examples of how these definitions are appropriate.
3. What is said to be the only way to handle sin? Find the verses in Romans 6 which support this idea.
4. What is "reconciliation"?
5. What is the difference between an apology and repentance?
6. Forgiveness is dependent on what actions on the part of the offender and the offended?

10

"MORE CONFUSING THAN AMUSING"

WRATH

"God forbid that I should glory, save in the cross of our Lord Jesus Christ." The most insidious heresy is advanced when we create a God to suit us. God can be heartbroken over sin (Hebrews 10:26–31; 12:28, 29; the entire Bible). The ultimate sin is to tell God how He ought to be. New interpretations now tell us that God does not have anger, but anguish. Not so!

A holy God is a God of wrath. The word "wrath" appears 189 times in the Scriptures. "Wrath" is used in the Bible even more than "grace." People today may cringe at the word, but without wrath there is no need for grace. To lessen judgment is to minimize sin. God has wrath, fierce wrath, great wrath, and a day of wrath. Love demands wrath, but wrath is satisfied by love. Wrath and love go together. They must not be separated. Love restrains wrath but does not swallow it. God has made promises. Some are positive; some are negative. God keeps *both*!

Modern interpretations also maintain that Jesus had no temper, that Christianity condemns *all* anger. Read the Gospel Accounts. Jesus had a temper! As Jesus cleansed the temple, He was not laughing and singing. God has a temper. Ask Adam and Eve, Noah, Babylon, Sodom and Gomorrah, Ananias and Sapphira! Romans is about grace, but it is even more about God's wrath.

(The word "wrath" appears twelve times in the book.) Paul, a disciple of grace, used the word "wrath" twenty-one times. "Wrath" is used more often than any other word in relation to God's judicial anger concerning the guilt of sin.

Why wrath? *Sin!* Wrath is severe anger. Can God be angry? The real question is "Why isn't God *more* angry?" Why would God put up with us? Would you? Why are we still alive? Sin is what God hates (Psalm 119:104). Every time we sin, we do what God hates. Sin is enmity against God, a mutiny, an insult. God gave man an incredible universe. Man treats it with contempt. Satan called God a liar (Genesis 3:3–5), and Eve believed Satan. What God hates, we now are.

With man, anger is a passion; with God, it is a principle. To some degree we know what sin does to man; we have no clue what it has done to God. God is the "Chief-Sufferer" in the universe. Sin nailed Jesus to the cross. God had reason for severe anger! If God could allow Jesus to be crucified, imagine what He can do to vile sinners! Man has anger toward anyone and anything that threatens or destroys what He loves. God is infinitely greater in law, justice, wrath, holiness, mercy, and goodness than we are. The more we sin, the less we know about it. Sin is against God (Psalm 51:4).

However, "wrath" is not God's final word. "Forgiveness" is. The unpardonable sin is to refuse to be forgiven.

REPENTANCE

God is "slow" to wrath (Proverbs 14:29; Nehemiah 9:17; James 1:19). However, every impenitent sinner and every sin will be punished. All that sinners can do is repent. Sin is radical. Repentance must be radical also. Guilt matters. By sinning, man casts out God. By repenting, man casts out self. Sinners must be delivered from sin and self. Therefore, the gospel must be "bad news" before it can be "good news." Repentance is the most difficult command.

All preachers in the Bible had but one topic: "repentance." John the Baptist had only one outline: "Repentance or Else." Jesus began His ministry by saying, "Repent and believe in the gospel" (Mark 1:15b). Forgiveness is impossible without repentance. John told flawed churches to repent (Revelation 2; 3). Even God cannot save sinners until they let Him. Tragically, the world is disoriented concerning repentance. Religious groups try to offer salvation without truth, knowledge, repentance, or obedience. Sinners are under the wrath of God. The world wants a Christianity that has low demands and no commands. Do not equate unmerited love with unconditional love. Who wants to repent? Behind every sin is unbelief (Hebrews 3:12–19). "Repentance" (Gk.: *metanoia*) is a second mind, a new mind, or a changed mind. Beliefs must be changed before behavior is changed. Changed lives are the fruit of repentance (Matthew 3:8).

Repentance is a spontaneous response to grace (2 Corinthians 7:9, 10; Romans 2:4). The prodigal returned home seeking to become an employee. His mind was right, but not his heart. The father's love changed that (Luke 15:17–24). Sinners must hate sin as God does. Christians live in faith and in repentance.

Things Connected to the Cross

Ephesians 5:21–32

". . . Christ also loved the church and gave Himself up for her, so that He might sanctify her, having cleansed her by the washing of water with the word" (Ephesians 5:25, 26).

God meets sinners only at the cross. The blessings of God are received upon God's terms—not ours. We must plant the cross in the middle of our hearts.

The cross is central; things connected to it are paramount. If you spend money to buy a suit, the good from that money comes from wearing the suit. Medicine can heal, but only when you take it. Medicine left in bottles is worthless. Paul said, ". . . not in cleverness of speech, so that the cross of Christ would not be made void [or lose its power]" (1 Corinthians 1:17). The power is there, but it must be connected.

THE NEW TESTAMENT

Jesus said, "For this is My blood of the covenant [testament], which is poured out for many for forgiveness of sins" (Matthew 26:28). The Bible is a book of blood. More than four hundred times, the Bible mentions "blood." Tragically, people today are too proud to associate with blood. It is too messy. Man could not write the Bible, and he would not if he could.

Too many think the cross of Christ was defeat and

His resurrection was victory. The New Testament only reveals *death* as the victory. Hebrews 9:15, 16 declares Jesus the mediator of the new covenant or testament. A testament (or will) is good only upon death. Jesus took the power of death from Satan through death. The resurrection validates the death! Jesus won at the cross. ". . . And He has taken it out of the way, having nailed it to the cross. When He had disarmed the rulers and authorities, He made a public display of them, having triumphed over them through Him" (Colossians 2:14, 15).

Jesus is the key to the Scriptures. You can find Jesus implied in every verse. To know Jesus, read the Bible, not some theological study by man. The "Living Word" is only found in the "Written Word."

It always amuses me how people are labeled according to their religious opinions. These labels are not biblical words. I just want to be a Christian, *period*! The issue is authority: Will we go by the Bible or not? I only want to be a member of Christ's church . . . no more, no less. Would you have liked to be a member of the first-century church? You can!

THE NEW TESTAMENT CHURCH

The Gospels focus upon Jesus; Acts through Revelation focus upon His church. Jesus promised Peter that He would build His church (Matthew 16:13–20). Jesus purchased the church with His own blood (Acts 20:28). He loved the church and gave Himself for it (Ephesians 5:22–30). Just like a husband ought to love his wife, Jesus loved the church and gave Himself that He might present to Himself a glorious church at the end of time (vv. 25–27). The benefits of His blood come in, through, and by His church. You cannot separate Christ from His church. The physical body of Christ purchased the spiritual body of Christ. The church is "God's forever family." Nothing on earth is like the church. Nothing on earth can do what the local church does when it is doing right. All that Jesus left upon the earth was His church. He did not die for man-made denominations. Christ is head over all things to the church, which is His body (Ephesians 1:22, 23; Colossians 1:18). Unity and equality are only found in God's church. Jesus broke down the wall, reconciling both to God in one body through the cross (Ephesians 2:13–22). The church is one, not many.

You may say, "But the church cannot save you!" Correct! Christ is the Savior—the church is the saved. The saved were added to the church (Acts 2:41–47). If you are saved, you have been added; if you have been added, you are saved. God does not forget. *There are no saved people outside the church.* When you preach Christ, you get the church. The church is universal, but the only way to contact the church is through a local congregation. The local church is the only stable, secure place on earth.

Some say, "I'm against organized religion!" Then you must be for "disorganized religion." I have also heard, "I love Christ, but I reject the church." This is neither scriptural nor sensible. My greatest joy is my wife. I would rather hear you compliment my wife than me. I will not even verbally defend myself—but you had better not harm her! I do not wish to stand before God having harmed Christ's church, His bride! Christ is going to present to Himself a glorious church not having spot or wrinkle or any such thing (Ephesians 5:27).

THE LORD'S DAY,
THE LORD'S SUPPER

Jesus is Lord. Culture cries, "Love, love, love," while refusing to define "love." Culture cries, "Believe in believing." This makes belief a human work! Believe what? Believe in whom? Someone says, "It doesn't make any difference what you believe—just be good, honest, and sincere." If you are "good, honest, and sincere," then it matters what you believe! What is the latest culture cry? It is to say, "Jesus, Jesus, Jesus" or "Jesus is Lord." Jesus silenced that. He said, "Why do you call Me, 'Lord, Lord,' and do not do what I say?" (Luke 6:46); "Not everyone who says to Me, 'Lord, Lord' will enter the kingdom of heaven, but he who does the will of My Father who is in heaven will enter" (Matthew 7:21). He will say to these, "I never knew you" (Matthew 7:23).

The Lord's Supper connects with the cross. The early church steadfastly assembled every Lord's Day (Acts 2:42; 20:7; 1 Corinthians 16:1, 2; Hebrews 10:25; Revelation 2:10). The Lord's Supper was placed in the assembly. The Christian does not partake alone and then assemble. The church is saved because the church has a Savior! Jesus is the host, not the guest! The Lord's Supper is not a church sacrament that forgives us—it is a memorial declaring that we are the forgiven. Jesus only has one command: "Follow Me." He only has one request: "Remember Me" (Matthew 26:26–29; 1 Corinthians 10:16; 11:23–26). One Bible, one bread, one cup, one body, one blood, and one covenant. The Lord's Supper every Lord's Day! The unleavened bread and the fruit of the vine! It would be worse than an insult—it would be blasphemy—to substitute anything for the bread and the cup. The church that does not meet cannot survive. As a community, the church has a life of its own (Acts 2:42).

The church does not grow on religious holidays, but it does grow on the Lord's Supper! To fail here is to make the church weak and sickly (1 Corinthians 11:23–30). The Lord's Supper is the greatest memorial on earth. Every member can participate. The focus is on the Word, the cross, and the table! Members examine themselves. Members "proclaim the Lord's death until He comes" (1 Corinthians 11:26). This is why we take the Lord's Supper to those who are unable to leave their homes. They, too, are part of the body. The Lord's Supper is a "celebration," not a funeral. It is the one memorial around which the church rallies!

BAPTISM

The cross must be placed again at the center of society and not just on the steeple of a church building. Jesus was not crucified in a cathedral between two candles, but on a cross between two thieves. All of us must raise (and answer) the question "What must I do to be saved?" Some suggest "The Sinner's Prayer," based on Luke 18:9–14, when the tax collector prayed, "God, be merciful to me, the sinner!" To offer this as a way to salvation exposes ignorance, dishonesty, or both. In this story, both the Pharisee and the tax collector were Jewish brethren at the temple. Neither was an alien sinner. One was proud; the other was contrite. This is the lesson. This parable of Jesus was before the cross, the Great Commission, the gospel, the Book of Acts, the Day of Pentecost, and the church. This was not about salvation. Jesus was not known, needed, or mentioned in this parable! Jesus is not in "The Sinner's Prayer."

Baptism connects sinners with the cross. In this act

we contact the blood of Jesus. It is the only place on earth where a non-Christian can. Therefore, it must not be reduced to a meaningless church ritual.

No religious word upsets people more than "baptism." If baptism is useless, why get angry? The fact is that a non-baptized Christian is foreign to the Scriptures and to the history of the first-century church. Baptism is an important event in salvation. Jesus put baptism in the Great Commission (Mark 16:15, 16). Sinners are baptized into the name of the Father, the Son, and the Holy Spirit (Matthew 28:18–20). The heart of the gospel is the death, burial, and resurrection of Christ (1 Corinthians 15:1–4). Sinners are baptized into the death, burial, and resurrection (Romans 6:3–6; Colossians 2:12). In baptism one accepts the Lord and is clothed with Him (Galatians 3:26–28). In scriptural baptism a sinner becomes a Christian (Acts 2:38).

Baptism is not a meritorious work of man, but the work of God. Each sinner must hear, believe, repent, and confess. No one could do these things for me, but someone else had to baptize me! Sinners, literally, "receive baptism." Twelve men were "rebaptized by Paul" in Ephesus (Acts 19:1–7).

Baptism saves (1 Peter 3:20, 21). The Jews on the Day of Pentecost needed to be baptized (Acts 2). The Ethiopian nobleman needed to be baptized (Acts 8:26–40). Paul needed to be baptized (Acts 9; 22:16). Cornelius needed to be baptized (Acts 10). You need to be baptized!

THE CRUCIFIED LIFE

The cross results in the crucified life. "I have been crucified with Christ; and it is no longer I who live, but Christ lives in me . . ." (Galatians 2:20, 21). Jesus was not on the cross six hours, but thirty-three years. He lived the life before He died the death. Salvation is free, but it costs us everything—our lives! In the historical sense, Jesus is risen; but in the holy sense, He is still on the cross. Christianity is a cross, not a crutch. The church was brought into existence through the cross and lives as an expression of the cross. Jesus calls us to die. Paul died daily (1 Corinthians 15:31). We come to the cross; we live at the cross. Paul said it best:

> Therefore if you have been raised up with Christ, keep seeking the things above, where Christ is, seated at the right hand of God. Set your mind on the things above, not on the things that are on earth. For you have died and your life is hidden with Christ in God. When Christ, who is our life, is revealed, then you also will be revealed with Him in glory (Colossians 3:1–4).

The crucified Savior can only be communicated by crucified servants. The church can only learn how to live when it has the courage to die. The church must never be more like the world that He came to save than the Christ who died to save the world. We cannot drink the cup of the Lord and the cup of demons (1 Corinthians 10:21). All the Bible that one has is what he lives.

> Give God the first hour of the day.
> Give God the first day of the week.
> Give God the first portion of your pay.
> Give God the first place in your heart.

When you undermine the book of blood, the blood-bought church, the Lord's Supper of remembrance, or baptism, nothing remains to connect you with the cross. Tragically, we have under-preached Jesus!

The cross . . .
there is no other way!

QUESTIONS FOR STUDY AND DISCUSSION

1. How do people "create" a god or gods to suit their own needs and desires?
2. Do you agree with how God is portrayed? Explain.
3. Discuss the meaning and importance of "repentance."
4. What does it mean to be "connected" to the cross?
5. What is the focus of the Gospels? What is the focus of Acts through Revelation?
6. Discuss the importance of the local church.
7. How is baptism connected to the cross?
8. How is the Lord's Supper connected to the cross?

11

"MORE CONFUSING THAN AMUSING"

SANCTIFICATION

"God forbid that I should glory, save in the cross of our Lord Jesus Christ." The church exists to save sinners and make saints (Matthew 28:18–20). However, evangelism, once "in," is now "out." "Why try to save someone who is not viewed as lost?" we now say.

Sanctification has never been "in." Most alleged Christians do not even know what it is. "Sanctification," simply, is being "set aside, dedicated." In religion, it means "holy." ". . . it is written, 'you shall be holy, for I am holy'" (1 Peter 1:15, 16). You cannot get the church right until you get the theology right. You can be right without being righteous (Matthew 6:1–18), but you cannot be righteous without being right. Sinners must be saved, and the saved must be sanctified.

We were saved (that is salvation). We are being saved (that is sanctification). We will be saved (that is glorification). The saved need to be sanctified, not re-saved. God cannot sanctify the unsaved. Salvation is positional (in Christ). Sanctification is a process. Salvation comes in a moment; sanctification takes a lifetime. "But we all, with unveiled face, beholding as in a mirror the glory of the Lord, are being transformed into the same image from glory to glory, just as by the Spirit of the Lord" (2 Corinthians 3:18; NKJV).

Let us not confuse salvation, sanctification, and glorification. We must learn to think in concepts. Most religious confusion comes from mixing up these three things. Salvation is not an initial spasm followed by chronic inertia.

FAITH, NOT PERFECTION
Can you be a Christian without being perfect? That is a good question! People say, "I tried and failed, so I quit." Extremes come from misunderstanding concepts. "Once saved, always saved" is wrong. "Once saved, never saved" is equally wrong! Christians must know they are saved (1 John 5:11–13). I cannot be perfect; therefore, I must be saved by faith. I cannot be perfect one minute, but I can be faithful one day at a time (Romans 3:10, 23). Faith works! (Hebrews 11). I cannot save myself by myself, so I must trust Jesus to save me. Our faith does not save us; the object of our faith (Jesus) saves us.

Saints sin! We sin because we are sinners. Even saints walking in the light sin (1 John 1:7—2:3). The blood of Christ saved us; the blood of Christ sanctifies us (Hebrews 10:29). Saints are constantly washed. Saints are saved—they have a Savior! There was a law system; saints now live in a faith system. The most practical thing on earth is faith. We walk by faith (not perfection; 2 Corinthians 5:7). "The righteous man shall live by faith" (read Habakkuk 2:4; Romans 1:17b; Galatians 3:11b; Hebrews 10:38a). Take notice when God quotes Himself!

The troubled "church of God at Corinth" was sanctified (1 Corinthians 1:2). As vile sinners, they had repented and were washed (1 Corinthians 6:9–11). Truth sanctifies (John 17:17, 19). Prayer sanctifies (1 Timothy 4:5). The Holy Spirit sanctifies (Romans 15:16; 1 Peter 1:2). Christ sanctifies (1 Corinthians 1:30; Hebrews 2:11). Jesus made one sacrifice once for all (Hebrews 10:10, 14, 16–24, 29; see also Hebrews 7—9). God sanctifies (John 10:36; 1 Thessalonians 5:23). Faith sanctifies (Acts 26:18). What is the conclusion? There were no saints in Corinth outside the church. Jesus cannot be our Savior until we obey Him as Lord. Jesus did not save us to leave us as we were. There must be a connection between believing and behaving. Saints must live in repentance. Saints are "saints," not "perfect angels."

Sanctification is discipleship. We have the mind of Christ (Philippians 2:5–11). We daily buffet our bodies (1 Corinthians 9:23–27). We put off the old and put on the new (2 Corinthians 5:17; Ephesians 4:22–24). We grow in grace and knowledge of Jesus (2 Peter 3:18). Jesus is formed in us (Galatians 4:19). Every thought becomes captive to Him (2 Corinthians 10:5). We possess our souls (1 Thessalonians 4:3–5). We "stimulate each other to love and good deeds" (Hebrews 10:24). There are no spiritual hermits. God makes His church out of saints. You cannot become a "spiritual giant" alone. We are all part of the body. There are no "Lone Ranger" Christians. We do not withdraw—we serve as His body. We deny ourselves and take up our crosses daily (Luke 9:23–26).

The twentieth-century theologian Reinhold Niebuhr wrote:

> Nothing that is worth doing can be achieved in our lifetime; therefore we must be saved by hope. Nothing . . . makes complete sense in any immediate context of history; therefore we must be saved by faith. Nothing we do, however virtuous, can be accomplished alone; therefore we are saved by love.[1]

---

[1] Reinhold Niebuhr, *The Irony of American History* (New York: Charles Scribner's Sons, 1952), 63.

Preaching the Cross

1 Corinthians 1:17–25; 2:1–5; 2 Corinthians 4:7;
1 Timothy 3:15, 16; 4:11–16; 2 Timothy 4:1–5

"For the word of the cross is foolishness to those who are
perishing, but to us who are being saved it is the power of God"
(1 Corinthians 1:18).

"As goes the pulpit, so goes the church!" God has but one Son, and He sent Him as a preacher. Preaching is divine. It originated with God, not man. The heart of the Great Commission is preaching (Mark 16:15, 16). The church began, grew, and continued with preaching (Acts 2; 8:4, 5; 10; 13; 20). Preaching made conversions; conversions made more preaching. New converts make more converts. When you get out of preaching, you get out of conversions. God uses only preaching to save sinners; God uses only preaching to keep the saved saved. God addresses human problems through preaching. An empty, deserted church building reveals that the church has quit preaching. Fill the pulpit, and you can fill the pews.

The church has never had more activities, yet the church has less and less preaching. The church is doing everything but preaching. A speaking God demands listening ears. We are saved by hearing, not by seeing (Romans 10:13–17). The central, primary, decisive function of the church is preaching. It is the facet in worship that represents God. We must ask, "Is there a message from the Lord?" Brethren sing, pray, fellowship, and commune; but God preaches. Some of our adult children never heard preaching when they were young! We must preach the gospel to ourselves every day, and we must continually preach it to our children!

Jesus had the original preacher school. He made preachers out of His apostles. The unique work of God is "to raise the dead" (Ephesians 2:1–5). Preachers are given thirty minutes each week "to raise the dead." We have under-preached Jesus! The world is not listening because the church is not talking. Nothing is more harmful than harmless preachers. The church must return to preaching!

REAL PREACHING

We have so corrupted love that we have to say "tough love." Those who promote love never attempt to define it. We have so emptied preaching that we must say "real preaching" when we talk about it. It requires a "real preacher" to have "real preaching." Without an education, miracles, a church building, or even an introduction, John the Baptist turned Israel upside down with preaching. I do not prepare sermons; I prepare Hodge. Only preachers preach! This is why preaching is the most difficult thing on earth to do. You are to be heard, yet not heard. If all the audience hears is the preacher, then the preacher has failed. After five minutes the audience must be unaware of the speaker. "Put yourself into it. Keep yourself out of it." "Real preaching" allows hearers to hear the voice of God!

Churches must be "preacher factories." We ought to have a surplus of preachers. Every preacher must die to the subconscious desire to please people.

Where have all the preachers gone? We have speakers, promoters, storytellers, psychologists, entertainers, clowns, politicians, church managers . . . everything but preachers. Religious pabulum can only result in spiritual malnutrition. God's sheep must not starve at the Master's table. Where could John the Baptist preach today? When we make converts, there will be no shortage of preachers.

Where could Paul preach? Read his resume:

> Serving the Lord with all humility and with many tears . . . teaching you publicly and from house to house. . . . But I do not consider my life of any account as dear to myself . . . to testify solemnly of the gospel of the grace of God. . . . Therefore, I testify to you this day that I am innocent of the blood of all men. For I did not shrink from declaring to you the whole purpose of God . . . (Acts 20:19–35; NKJV).

Paul was a real preacher!

Movie directors were discussing movies. They agreed that stars today are not on the same level as stars of the past. One concluded, "We used to make movies for adults. Now we make movies for adolescents." Could a similar situation exist in the church? Do our sermons confront adults or please children? It takes a man to preach. "Wimps" need not apply. Preaching is not "kid stuff." Preaching caused John the Baptist to be jailed and Jesus to be crucified. In preaching, God confronts man in sin. This is painful, yet necessary! No wonder prophets have always been stoned (Matthew 23:37)!

True preaching, by itself, does not save. It is the content, the message that saves (1 Corinthians 1:21). This is not an "either/or" situation, but "both/and." Both preaching *and* the message must be involved. Silence cannot save! The glorious message is harmless on a library shelf or placed upon a coffee table. In Acts the church grew as the gospel spread. God speaks and acts. God calls preachers to speak and act to cause disciples to speak and act.

God does things differently. Man displays riches with riches. Diamonds are displayed on velvet by men wearing white gloves. The glorious gospel (the "treasure") is preached by clay pots ("earthen vessels"; 2 Corinthians 4:7). Who is Paul? Who is Apollos? They are nothing (1 Corinthians 3:4–7)! God is everything! Again, this is a main factor in the difficulty of preaching. Preachers must "give it all they have" without being the focus of the sermon. Paul said, "For if I preach the gospel, I have nothing to boast of, for I am under compulsion; for woe is me if I do not preach the gospel" (1 Corinthians 9:16).

A prayer from a past generation was correct: "May the preacher hide himself behind the cross." Amen! Preaching is an awesome responsibility! It must be far more than a nice man suggesting to nice people that they must be nicer. God confronts sinners in preaching. You cannot build a church where preachers are not allowed to speak boldly. Preachers do not debate; they declare! (Acts 20:27). Paul wrote, "For the love of Christ controls us" (2 Corinthians 5:14a). The world is lost in sin. What does God want us to do? *Preach!*

PREACHING THE GOSPEL
God saves the world through the preached message

(the gospel; 1 Corinthians 1:21). What is the gospel? Most think they know, but few do! What is it? The gospel is not issues, pet peeves, doctrine in general, hobbies, creeds, or "concordance preaching." "Concordance preaching" may teach facts, but it does not always contain the gospel. You can quote a hundred Scriptures without preaching the gospel.

The gospel is the "big picture." In art class you learn, "Paint the blue sky first." The gospel is "God's big picture." "For I delivered to you as of first importance what I also received, that Christ died for our sins according to the Scriptures, and that He was buried, and that He was raised on the third day according to the Scriptures" (1 Corinthians 15:3, 4). This gospel must permeate our entire lives. The crucified life is the only life. Tell people what God did before you tell them what to do. Start with God's love for you, not your love for God. Grace can easily demand works, but works leave no place for grace. Do not turn the "good news" into "bad news." Sermons can be full of biblical texts but empty of the gospel. People are called to obey the gospel, not law (2 Thessalonians 1:7–9). There cannot be "another gospel" (Galatians 1:6–12). All preaching, in some sense, must be gospel preaching.

We claim to be "gospel preachers," but are we? The gospel that Jesus brought is the most powerful thing to come to earth. Who, other than God, could turn an instrument of death into the world's most magnetic power? "'And I, if I am lifted up from the earth, will draw all men to Myself.' But He was saying this to indicate the kind of death by which He was to die" (John 12:32, 33). Paul preached a Christ who stands forever crucified (1 Corinthians 2:1, 2). We proclaim the Lord's death until He comes (1 Corinthians 11:26). The heart and soul of apostolic preaching was the cross. The only permanent motivation is the cross. When the cross ceases to touch us, nothing can. Preachers must never be "too big" to preach the simple gospel. People cannot obey a gospel they have never heard! Bring sinners to the cross and leave them there! Perfect people do not need preaching; the rest of us do! Reformists in England during the eighteenth century believed the gospel could alter the social fabric of England. It did! There will be enough Christians reading this book to change the direction of our nation if they take God seriously! That is the awesome power of the gospel!

THE SIN ISSUE

The gospel is "good news"; sin is "bad news." If sin is harmless, then the gospel is useless. Heaven is real, but in one sense, it is a fringe benefit. People want heaven to be like a vacation. No sin can enter heaven. Man is lost, damned in his sins. Man does not just need to be saved— he has a Savior. We have neglected to teach the enormity of sin! Sin alienated us from God (Isaiah 59:1, 2). God cannot touch sin! Everything sin touches dies. The soul who sins dies (Ezekiel 18:4, 20). The wages of sin is death (Romans 6:23). Sinners must deal with their sins before they even consider heaven. Forgiveness of sins restores us to God. Heaven is where God and Jesus are. Too many wish to avoid hell, to escape punishment, rather than desiring to be restored to God.

The Bible talks about the offense of the cross (Galatians 5:11). Nothing offends people like the preaching of the gospel! The whole idea of "gospel" counters human thought. The Jews thought the Messiah would come on a stallion, leading them to military triumph. Jesus rode into Jerusalem on a donkey in order to be crucified. Man does not wish to be told there is something wrong with him. He refuses to acknowledge helplessness. He refuses to be a clay pot with no intrinsic value. It is one thing to be saved by grace; it is another thing to be paralyzed by it. Action results from grace, but actions are no substitute for grace. No man can stand at the cross and boast of his own achievements. The gospel shatters all human ability.

Jesus is "the Lamb slain from the foundation of the world" (Revelation 13:8; NKJV). A lamb? What good is that? This is why the gospel sounds good only to bad, sinful, lost people. "Old-fashioned sin" is "out." We must bring back an understanding of sin by preaching. What causes a sinner to repent? The cross! Apart from the cross, there is no power to die to self. Preaching will either offend man or God.

The cross of shame became the throne of glory. Do not equate being positive with preaching truth. Never confuse our desire for people to accept the gospel with creating a gospel that is acceptable to people. The cross asks us to die. The only way to handle sin is to die to it. How dare we accept sin when God has declared a holy war against it!

PASSION

The only man-made things in heaven are the scars of Jesus Christ! How dare any man preach *the Passion* without passion! The gospel can only be preached urgently and with authority (Titus 2:15). Preaching with passion demands a verdict. The cross appeals to our understanding, our deepest emotions, our dignity as human beings, and our moral obligations. It presents the only way to live. The only thing Jesus hands out is crosses: "If anyone wishes to come after Me, he must deny himself, and take up his cross daily and follow Me. For whoever wishes to save his life will lose it, but whoever loses his life for My sake, he is the one who will save it" (Luke 9:23, 24; see Matthew 16:24, 25; Mark 8:34, 35).

Christianity is essentially aggressive and evangelistic. It lives to refute false religions. No compromises are proposed; no treaties are signed. The gospel is the only true religion. It demands acceptance and obedience from all sinners! Preach it!

The cross . . .
there is no other way!

QUESTIONS FOR STUDY AND DISCUSSION

1. Why does the church exist?
2. Discuss the difficulty people seem to have with the idea that saints sin.
3. React to the statement "As goes the pulpit, so goes the church."
4. Define "gospel." What approach does the author suggest for preaching the gospel?
5. What provides the power for a sinner to repent or a Christian to "die to self"? Explain.
6. What is the difference in desiring that people accept the gospel and desiring to present a gospel that people will accept?
7. How important is faithful preaching?

12

"MORE CONFUSING THAN AMUSING"

THE INCARNATION

"God forbid that I should glory, save in the cross of our Lord Jesus Christ." My head aches at the thought of the incarnation! Man wants to be God—that, I understand. What I cannot understand is that the sovereign, infinite, immutable, eternal God became man . . . in diapers! Only God could think of this! Only He could do this! "In the beginning was the Word, and the Word was with God, and the Word was God"; "And the Word became flesh, and dwelt among us" (John 1:1, 14a). Jesus is the *only* mediator between God and man (1 Timothy 2:5, 6). He is the living bread from heaven (John 6:48–58). On the holy mountain God said, "This is My beloved Son, with whom I am well-pleased; listen to Him!" (Matthew 17:5; see 2 Peter 1:17). The incarnation is the "miracle of miracles."

> The heavenly Son of an earthen mother,
> The earthly Son of a heavenly Father,
> So divine, not human,
> So human, not divine.

Jesus Christ could not be invented. God wrapped the truth in Jesus and sent the Man! God's ultimate, final revelation is in Christ (Hebrews 1:1–3; Romans 1:1–6). Jesus never rebuked anyone who called Him God or worshiped Him. The coming of Christ is the heart of the

Scriptures. Jesus is the *Logos*—the Living Word of God. We believe that Jesus is God, but we must also believe that God is Jesus!

Christianity is essentially historical. It is not "the myth among myths," an allegory without substance. The doctrine of the cross is not just that there is life after death, but that there is life instead of death. Jesus is the way that man was intended to live. Paul's favorite expression was "in Christ"; he used variations of it 135 times in his writings. If we can get Christ into us, He will find a way to bring Himself out of us! Jesus is a *Person*, not a *program*! God gave us Christ; we give back to Him Christlike lives!

THE VIRGIN BIRTH

The divinity of Jesus is unavoidably connected with His virgin birth (Matthew 1:18–25). If both parents of Jesus had been human, then His blood would have been as worthless as ours. He could not have resurrected Himself or anyone else. Our beloved Hugo McCord said, "Christianity without the virgin birth becomes a religion without salvation by the blood and without a resurrection. It is reduced simply to a social gospel for this life only."[1]

Man probably stumbles more over Christ's humanity than His divinity. While human, Jesus did not merely go through the motions, as if performing in a play on a stage. In the garden that was real sweat dropping like blood (Luke 22:44). His favorite title for Himself was "Son of Man," which is found more than eighty times in the

---

[1]Hugo McCord, "Jesus: Our Eternal Savior," in "Jesus Christ, the Divine Son of God," *Truth for Today* (May 2000): 6.

New Testament. The divinity of Jesus is best demonstrated by His humanity. We greet good news with skepticism, yet bad news we swallow at once. You do not have to prove absolute truth. Absolute truth proves itself. God is not running to be elected God. The prime needs of religion today are doctrine, theology, and truth!

JESUS IS LORD

That Jesus is Lord is so simple, yet so profound! We pray to God, whom we cannot see, and expect to go to heaven on the virtue of His Son. The way up is down; we empty ourselves to be full. We confess being wrong to be made right. The strongest are the weakest; the poorest, the richest. We die to live and give to get. At the same time, we confound the critics with our unbelievable practicality. The middle cross at Calvary was not Christ's—it was mine. Dying was His reason for living. The entire emphasis of John's Gospel Account is the eternal significance of Jesus. The power to live the Epistles is found in the Gospels. Jesus was a "man's man," not a weakling!

"Amazing grace." Jesus was not God, then the God-man, and then God-only again when He returned to heaven! In the incarnation Jesus eternally connected Himself with humanity. I was never God and never will be God! Jesus was *both* totally humbled and totally exalted. His exaltation did not destroy His humanity; rather, it glorified His humanity. Jesus is the firstborn from the dead (Colossians 1:15–20). He is the first fruits of those who sleep (1 Corinthians 15:20, 23). Christ's church is made up of "the firstborn ones." I only want to be a member of the body that carries on His life.

"O God, Make Me Like Jesus"

Matthew 28; Mark 16;
Luke 24; John 20; 21

"Beloved, now we are children of God, and it has not appeared as yet what we will be. We know that when He appears, we will be like Him, because we will see Him just as He is" (1 John 3:2).

Resurrection! This is the defining difference that sets Christianity apart from all other religions! It has been said if there had been no resurrection, our world today would never have heard of Jesus. Angels asked, "Why do you seek the living One among the dead? He is not here, but He has risen" (Luke 24:5b, 6a). Jesus was not resuscitated, reincarnated, or recreated; He was resurrected. He went "through death and out the other side into a new world, a world of new and deathless creation, still physical only somehow transformed."[2] Christianity claims that something happened to Jesus which had not happened to anyone else. Our Christian hope is not just immortality of the soul but the resurrection and transformation of our bodies.

---

[2]N. T. (Tom) Wright, *Luke for Everyone* (Louisville, Ky.: Westminster John Knox Press, 2004), 296–97.

Most religions have holy places; Christianity does not. Other religions have tombs; Christianity does not. Of what use is a "dead Savior"?

No man witnessed the resurrection. Who *was* there? Was God there? God did resurrect Jesus.[3] Was the Holy Spirit there? Jesus was raised by the Spirit (Romans 8:10, 11). Were angels there? We do not know. Man was not! Christians believe because of an empty tomb! Christianity stands or falls upon an empty tomb! One bone found would totally destroy Christianity! Paul said, "That I may know Him and the power of His resurrection" (Philippians 3:10a). Jesus physically died and literally was resurrected. This means that He is alive today. It also means that we can believe in and obey Him today. This is the gospel! The Christian hope is not life after death, but life, *period*! He said, "I am the resurrection and the life . . ." (John 11:25, 26); "I am the way, and the truth, and the life" (John 14:6a). Resurrection faith is built upon resurrection fact.

Nothing is more fatal to the Christian faith than to locate its meaning outside its happening. The resurrection is without meaning unless it really happened. The blasphemous Jesus Seminar said that the resurrection of Jesus Christ had nothing to do with his corpse. How silly can one get? Jesus is not a liar, a hoax, or a fraud. The cross is not fiction; it is not a myth or an allegory. His death and burial were real. His resurrection was real. Jesus is historical. An expert in myths studied himself into faith and said, "These things really happened. I know what myth is . . . this

---

[3]See Acts 2:24, 32, 36; 3:15, 26; 4:10; 5:30; 10:40; 13:30, 33, 34; 17:31; Romans 10:9; 1 Corinthians 6:14; 2 Corinthians 4:14; Galatians 1:1; Ephesians 1:20.

is not myth." Christians do not have a cemetery or a tomb because Christ's tomb is empty. No one denied that His tomb was empty!

THE BURIAL

The gospel is the death, *burial*, and resurrection of Christ (1 Corinthians 15:1–4). We preach the death and the resurrection, but we skip the burial. A burial demands a death. Skeptics have the fairy tale that Jesus fainted, was in a coma, or was in a trance, and that He fooled the authorities. Angels pointed out where Jesus' corpse was placed (Matthew 28:6; Mark 16:6). Resurrection demands a death, a burial. A burial demands a body.

Baptism is a burial into the death, burial, and resurrection of Christ (Romans 6:1–5; Colossians 2:12). A sinner's greatest burial is to be buried by baptism with and into Christ! The burial shouted, "All is lost. Death has won; life has lost." The situation may have seemed bleak on Friday, but Sunday was coming!

INFALLIBLE PROOFS

"To these He also presented Himself alive after His suffering, by many convincing proofs, appearing to them over a period of forty days and speaking of the things concerning the kingdom of God" (Acts 1:3). Christianity is built upon the empty tomb. If Jesus cannot do anything about death, then whatever else He does amounts to nothing. "Why do you seek the living One among the dead? He is not here, but He has risen," an angel said (Luke 24:5b, 6a). The Book of Acts does not debate the resurrection—it declares it! A dead Savior did not produce Christianity. The resurrection is the most certified fact in all history. Lyman Abbott said, "The resurrection of Jesus Christ is the best attested fact in history."[4]

Jewish law refused circumstantial evidence. The verdict came from two or more witnesses (2 Corinthians 13:1). The gospel is the death, burial, and resurrection (1 Corinthians 15:1–4). Keep reading. God gave additional space in the Scriptures to the witnesses. The resurrection will stand in any court of law.

(1) *The apostle Paul.* The conversion of Saul (Paul) is enough to certify the resurrection. The persecutor became the preacher! Why? He saw the risen Savior (1 Corinthians 9:1; 15:8–11). He had no doubts. He died for his faith and for his preaching. Paul believed in and preached a bodily resurrection.

(2) *The enemies.* Paradoxically, enemies believed when disciples doubted. They warned Pilate that Jesus promised a resurrection in three days. Pilate said, ". . . make [the tomb] as secure as you know how" (Matthew 27:65). A huge stone was rolled over the entrance and sealed. Soldiers were put in place to guard the tomb. Humanly speaking, man could not have removed the body.

When the rock was rolled aside, exposing the empty tomb, no one shouted, "Find that body!" The Jewish leaders, Roman soldiers, Pharisees, Pilate, and Herod did not go from house to house in search of the body. They knew Jesus was resurrected! They immediately tried to squelch the news. The rock at the tomb was not rolled aside to allow Jesus to exit, but to allow man to enter. Jesus' enemies knew that a corpse could not be found!

Throughout history no skeptic, Jew, or Roman has claimed to have found Jesus' body. The silence is stagger-

[4]Lyman Abbott, *The Theology of an Evolutionist* (New York: Outlook Co., 1925), 129.

ing! Disposing of a human body without a trace would be a miracle itself. When Peter preached that first sermon (Acts 2), he was in close proximity to that cemetery. Three thousand people from everywhere obeyed his resurrection message: "Therefore let all the house of Israel know for certain that God has made Him both Lord and Christ—this Jesus whom you crucified" (Acts 2:36). Skeptics have to face this question: "What happened to that body?" There are more verses in the Bible on the resurrection than on Jesus' birth.

(3) *The apostles.* Cowards became martyrs! What can explain this? The resurrection! Matthew, Mark, Luke, John, Peter, and Paul were competent witnesses. Would you brand them liars? Can you trust the Gospel Accounts in the Bible? Scholars call Luke an historian of the first rank. How can you explain the beginning, the growth, and the continued existence of the early church? It all arises from the resurrection!

(4) *The women.* Jesus appeared first to Mary Magdalene (Mark 16:9–11; John 20:1–18). The women came to visit a cemetery and bring flowers (Matthew 28:1–10). Honor them for this! Their testimony is made stronger when you realize that they never dared to imagine a resurrection. When, in joy, they found the apostles, the apostles laughed at them and refused to believe (Luke 24:11; Mark 16:11). Jesus rebuked the apostles for this (Mark 16:14). We cannot grasp the problem they had in believing. They were so focused upon finding a dead body that they could not recognize a living Savior!

(5) *The appearances.* Most scholars list ten resurrection appearances, while some list twelve:

- to Mary Magdalene (Mark 16:9–11; see John 20:1–18)

143

- to other women (Matthew 28:1–10)
- to two men on the Emmaus Road (Luke 24:13–32; see Mark 16:12)
- to Simon Peter (Luke 24:34)
- to ten apostles, without Thomas (John 20:19–25; see Mark 16:14; Luke 24:36–49)
- to eleven apostles, with Thomas (John 20:26–28)
- to seven disciples at the Sea of Galilee (John 21:1–23)
- to eleven apostles in Galilee (Matthew 28:16–20; see Mark 16:15–18)
- to more than five hundred brethren (1 Corinthians 15:6)
- to James (1 Corinthians 15:7)
- to eleven apostles (Luke 24:50–53)
- to Paul (1 Corinthians 15:8; see Acts 9; 26).

Notice that Jesus did not appear before His enemies—the religious Jews, Pilate, or Herod.

(6) *John.* John arrived at the tomb, stopped, and then followed Peter inside. When he saw the folded grave clothes, he put all the evidence together. He saw and believed (John 20:2–10).

(7) *"Doubting" Thomas* (John 20:24–29). Like the others, Thomas was devastated by the death of Jesus. God does not die! God in man did die. Thomas missed the first assembly (John 20:24). This failure could have been fatal to his soul. The disciples went after him. We must learn and practice this today (James 5:19, 20; Galatians 6:1, 2; Jude 22, 23). He was present the next time. Do not be too harsh with him. Have you ever seen a resurrected man? Would you believe such a claim? Thomas demanded the "finger test." Jesus welcomed it! Thomas declared, "My Lord and my God!" The witnesses have spoken!

GRAVEYARD HUMOR

The Bible is a fascinating book. Man could not have written it. He would not have written it if he could have. This fact is a powerful argument for inspiration.

(1) *The women.* The angels and Jesus appeared to women first! They came with spices. This was a beautiful gesture, but not a practical one. Then it occurred to them: Who would roll away the rock? Several strong men would have been needed, but it required one angel!

(2) *The soldiers.* Can there be anything more ludicrous than the Roman army guarding a tomb? There was an earthquake; then an angel rolled back the stone (Matthew 28:2). The guards became as dead men. Were they rebuked? Were they commanded, "Find that body"? Were they executed according to Roman custom? No! The chief priests bribed the soldiers at a great price (Matthew 28:11–15) to say that they had fallen asleep! Yet the price paid by a soldier found asleep on his watch was death!

(3) *The disciples on the Emmaus Road* (Luke 24:13–32). Jesus joined two devastated disciples as they walked. They were amazed that Jesus had "missed" everything that had been happening in Jerusalem. They were the ones who had missed it! Ironically, Jesus, using the Scriptures, preached the gospel to them. When Jesus blessed and broke the bread, they recognized Him. How many of us are missing the truth? If Christ is not risen, then our faith is empty (1 Corinthians 15:10–19).

RESURRECTION POWER

". . . that I may know Him and the power of His resurrection" (read Philippians 3:7–11). The heart and soul of the church is to seek and save the lost through the power of the gospel of a risen Lord. The cross was the victory won; the resurrection was the death accepted, validated, and endorsed by God. Death could not hold Jesus (Acts 2:22–36). In death Jesus defeated death. The cross marks the "death of death." Jesus freed us from the "sting" of death (1 Corinthians 15:54–57). Sinners are saved by Christ's death—not by His resurrection.

By His death, Jesus saved us from the law of sin and death (Romans 8:1, 2). To conquer sin is to eliminate death. Jesus appeared in heaven with His blood (Hebrews 10). He is "the resurrection and the life" (John 11:25, 26), not merely "immortality and life." Hell is immortal. Our souls are immortal. Jesus is "resurrection"! Paul promised our change (1 Corinthians 15:50–58). On the cross Jesus abolished death (2 Timothy 1:10). On the cross He took the power of death from Satan (2 Timothy 1:10). We are saved ". . . since a death has taken place" (Hebrews 9:15).

Jesus' resurrection guarantees ours. What God did in a Jerusalem cemetery for Jesus, He will do for us. We were not made to die, but to live. What is the doctrine, the hope of the resurrection, *right now*? Nothing on earth is irreversible! My life is not futile; it has a purpose. My failures are not fatal; they are forgiven. My death is not final; there is a resurrection. What a faith! What a hope! We will be like Jesus! When He was on the cross, Satan was defeated, sin was overcome, and death was abolished. "But thanks be to God, who gives us the victory through our Lord Jesus Christ" (1 Corinthians 15:57).

The cross . . .
there is no other way!

QUESTIONS FOR STUDY AND DISCUSSION

1. Explain the importance of the virgin birth of Christ.
2. Discuss Jesus' divinity and humanity before and after His life on earth. Why is this important?
3. What sets Christianity apart from every other world religion?
4. What evidence do we have that Jesus was resurrected?
5. List the resurrection appearances of Christ. Why do you think He chose to appear to these people in particular?
6. What is the great guarantee for Christians in Jesus' resurrection?

13

"MORE CONFUSING THAN AMUSING"

THE BLOOD

"God forbid that I should glory, save in the cross of our Lord Jesus Christ." A "holy hush" grasps us as we enter the "Holy of Holies" through the perfect blood of the Lamb (Hebrews 10:19). The Bible is a book about blood! People today are horrified by blood. Some claim that Christianity needs new symbols. This impugns the intelligence and the character of God! The Lamb of God is the center and centerpiece of all history (Revelation 13:8). The cross is the place where we hurt God the most; it also is where God loved us the most (John 3:16). Tragically, there are some seminaries where it is taboo to mention the blood of Christ. Have the people there forgotten what business they are in? The theology of heaven is Christ-centered, cross-centered, and blood-centered.

THE ENORMITY OF SIN
No book in all the Bible clashes more violently with the modern mind than *Leviticus*. How did this book get into the Bible? We usually skip it. This is where God detailed the sacrificial system. It is filled with priests, sacrifices, and blood! God, in that book of law, was teaching the exceeding sinfulness of sin (Romans 7:13). God and sin cannot mix. Sin contradicts God! Sin cannot be overlooked. Every sin and every impenitent sinner will be punished. Sin cannot be excused even by a divine

decree. Sin's sting is the sting of death (1 Corinthians 15:56). Forgiveness of sin can only come from the shedding of blood. Under the Law, remission of sin required blood (Hebrews 9:22). The Law is our teacher (Galatians 3:22–29; Romans 15:4; 1 Corinthians 10:11).

The sacrificial system, with the blood of bulls and goats, could not take away sin (Hebrews 10:4). Man could not keep the Law (Acts 15:8–11). The blood of mankind is worthless. What man could not do, God still did in man. Robert Coleman counted 460 specific references to blood in the Scriptures.[1] Jesus talked about His blood more than He spoke of His cross or His death. Christianity is a religion of blood. The blood of Christ created a "blood bank in heaven" that is always full. Jesus died for our sins according to the Scriptures (1 Corinthians 15:1–4).

The perfect blood reconciles (2 Corinthians 5:14–21), washes (Revelation 1:5; 7:14), redeems (Ephesians 1:7; 1 Peter 1:18, 19), cleanses (1 John 1:7), justifies (Romans 5:8, 9), overcomes (Revelation 12:11), sanctifies (Hebrews 10:10; 13:12), propitiates (1 John 2:2), and gives us peace (Colossians 1:20; Ephesians 2:13–16). The real, historical, full, and final payment for our sins is the blood of Christ. "Behold, the Lamb of God who takes away the sin of the world!" (John 1:29, 36).

THINGS CONNECTED TO THE BLOOD

The New Testament (or new covenant; Matthew 26:26–28; 1 Corinthians 11:25, 26; Hebrews 13:20). Every word in the New Testament drips with the blood of

---

[1]Robert Coleman, "The Gospel of Blood" (http://www.preaching.com/preaching/pastissues/robertcoleman.htm; Internet; accessed 1 December 2006).

Christ. When you read the Scriptures and fail to find Christ, you are misreading it. The blood of Abel cries out to God from the ground (Genesis 4:2–12; see Matthew 23:35; Luke 11:51). The blood of Jesus speaks of better things than does Abel's (Hebrews 12:24). "Listen" to the blood (Hebrews 9:11–22)!

The New Testament Church (Acts 20:28; Ephesians 5:25–28). Millions of sacrificial animals and birds shed their blood, but man was still mired in sin. Aren't you glad we are not under such a system today? Animal blood cannot buy anything. The blood of Christ bought only one thing—the church! Blood is identified with life; in losing one, you lose the other. The price is found in what was bought. The local church, with all its faults, is still the most powerful group on earth! To minimize the church is to denigrate the blood.

The Lord's Supper (Acts 2:42; 1 Corinthians 10:16–21; 11:24–30). There is one way, one body (the church), one bread, one blood, one supper, and one life! The blood is the fruit and the infinite power of the cross. The Lord's Supper proclaims Christ's death until He returns (1 Corinthians 11:26).

Baptism (Romans 6:1–5; Galatians 3:26, 27; Colossians 2:12). Three bear witness on earth—the Spirit, the water, and the blood (1 John 5:3–8). In baptism sinners are clothed with Christ on the cross. It is the blood that bestows upon us the right to heaven. The world wants salvation without the blood, without the Bible, without the church, without the Lord's Supper, and without baptism. It will not work!

My Cross

Matthew 10:37–39; 16:24–26; Mark 8:33–37;
Luke 9:23–25; 14:27; 15:25–32; Romans 6:1–11;
Galatians 2:20, 21; 6:14; Philippians 1:21

*"'And he who does not take his cross and follow after Me
is not worthy of Me'" (Matthew 10:38).*

What does Christianity have that other religions do not and cannot have? Jesus Christ and His cross! You cannot understand the cross until you stand under it. God cannot and will not save man apart from Christ and His cross.

If His cross was necessary, so is ours. For those who live in Christ, the judgment is already past. To those outside salvation, the judgment is yet to come. God has given us Jesus; we give Jesus back to God through Christ-like living. God will accept nothing else from us. Only Jesus can live the Christian life, and He does that through us. Jesus was not on the cross six hours; He was on that cross thirty-three years. Our salvation is not for a moment, but for a crucified lifetime.

There is no "cheap grace." Grace does not overlook, evade, forget, or repeal God's truth, wrath, or punishment. Grace absorbs the price, penalty, and punishment for sin. Every impenitent sinner and every sin is punished—either in Christ or in hell. The only thing Christ gives out is crosses; the only thing the church has to give out is crosses. The church, sadly, is giving out everything except crosses. Everything of God is in Christ, not out of Christ.

JESUS DIED

God, being God, cannot die—yet Jesus died! Concerning His death, we must know *that* He died and *why* He died (for our sins). Scholars are more interested in *how* He died. We know that Pilate was shocked at how quickly Jesus died (Mark 15:44). Still, he did not doubt that He was dead. The other two being crucified had to have their legs broken to bring their deaths (John 19:31–34). The Holy Spirit thought this was good information for us. Otherwise, it would not be part of the Scriptures. The Bible never says that Christ lived for us or worked for us, but the Bible emphatically declares that Jesus died for us.

Some think Jesus died from exhaustion. He had been put through a grueling experience. He had been deprived of sleep, barely fed, and brutalized in both Jewish and Roman trials. One scholar concluded that Jesus had walked 2.6 miles during these trials. Do not forget the harsh scourging. Pilate said, ". . . Behold, the Man!" (John 19:5). Exhausted, Jesus was unable to carry His cross. I *think* He chose when He would die; I *know* He chose when to be resurrected. Jesus had the power to lay down His life and the power to take it back (John 10:15–18). Jesus had control over His own execution. Having said, "It is finished!"—having met God's total demand—Jesus bowed His head and gave up His spirit (John 19:30).

The cross provides God's answer to the problem of sin. Some think Jesus died from a broken heart. Jesus was physically depleted. He was emotionally drained. His greatest agony was in Gethsemane. Luke tells us that His sweat became like drops of blood (Luke 22:44). Such is a rare phenomenon (called hematidrosis or hemohidrosis). Jesus was to receive God's holy anger poured out upon Him. An apostle had betrayed Him, another apostle had denied Him, and the remaining apostles had deserted Him. Humanly speaking, Jesus had been left alone. "He came to His own, and those who were His own did not receive Him" (John 1:11). He was crucified in God's chosen city, Jerusalem. Everything good that God wanted in man was violated at the cross. Jesus even rejected the mild analgesic offered early in the crucifixion process (Matthew 27:34).

Some think Jesus died from a ruptured heart. His quick death does indicate a catastrophic terminal event. He was crushed for our iniquities (Isaiah 53:5). Few men were more mistreated than Jesus. Whether He died of cardiac rupture or of cardiopulmonary failure, the vital fact is *that* He died, not *how* He died. Roman guards did not leave their victims until they were sure death had occurred. Jesus died!

JESUS DIED FOR ME

Pilate would not have released the body for burial unless he was sure Jesus was dead (Luke 23:50–56). Pilate never doubted that Jesus was dead. That Jesus died is historical (abstract). That Jesus died for me is personal (salvational). It is not enough to believe that Jesus died; I must believe that Jesus died for me! Everything Jesus did on the cross, He did for me! This is the gospel. Hear it! Believe it! Obey it (2 Thessalonians 1:8)! Preach it (Mark 16:15, 16)! God loves me! God wants me (John 3:16)! Sing it. . . . Shout it. . . . "I have a Savior!" The US has the Declaration of Independence; Christians have the Declaration of Dependence. Salvation is not something you do; it is Someone you receive (Matthew 11:28–30). All preaching, in some sense, must be gospel preaching.

> I have been saved.
> I am being saved.
> I will be saved.

Remember this: Preach the gospel to yourself every day. It took a cross to save us; it takes a cross to keep us saved. Ponder the sovereignty of grace.

> You cannot earn grace—it is a gift.
> You cannot buy grace—it is not for sale.
> You cannot merit grace—it is unmerited.
> You cannot repay grace—it creates no debt.
> Grace changes everything!

Jesus died for my sins (1 Corinthians 15:1–4)! A little girl heard a sermon on the cross. She told the preacher, "You must love Him more than anything else in this world, since He has done all that for you." Unmerited love is not unconditional; sinners cannot be saved remaining in the "far country" (Luke 15; KJV). Salvation is not by works of merit, yet Christian love is expressed in good works (Ephesians 2:8–10). Authentic love makes demands; its conditions are not for the childish. Christianity is a gift, not a bargain. It cost Jesus His life; it costs us ours. Grace is not a genie in a bottle; grace is a cross. Discipleship comes with an awesome price—your life. One thing that Jesus did not say on the cross is "Mine." Who crucified Christ? I did! Who nailed Jesus to the cross? I did! We cannot understand what Christ did for us until we grasp what we did to cause it! Sin is eternal and heinous; it separates us from God (Isaiah 59:1–3). Christ did for us what we could not do. Apart from Christ we can only die in our sin. Peter accused his audience of murdering Christ (Acts 2:22–36). They had done that physically; we have done it spiritually. We must grasp the depth of sin to accept the glory of grace. If people have not been converted to Christ, they may think they have tried Christianity and failed; in reality, they have not tried it at all. To give yourself and your children a future, give them a cross. The crucifixion explains the creation! Because of me it had to be.

MY CROSS

Jesus had His cross; I have mine. It is easy to promote His; it is also easy to neglect mine. If I do not accept mine, I cannot possess His. Unless I take up my cross, His is in vain. I may not be able to change the world, but God can change me. No one can walk the path of righteousness for me. I must sacrifice the "Big Me" to receive the "Great He." The only good in me is Christ in me (Galatians 2:20, 21). On the cross Jesus died *for* us, not merely *instead* of us. We, too, die, suffer, and carry our crosses. He bore His; we also bear ours. We have the gift of grace, but we also have the grit of good works. Grace is not earned, but it demands our effort. Salvation can never be "Come in, Savior, but stay out, Lord." Martin Luther King, Jr., well said, "The cross we bear precedes the crown we wear."[2] No one can boast at the foot of the cross. A cross around

[2]Martin Luther King, Jr., "Challenge to the Churches and Synagogues," *Challenge to Religion*, ed. Mathew Ahmann (Chicago: Henry Regnery Company, 1963), 168.

your neck can never substitute for a cross on your back.

REREAD—THINK—MEDITATE—ACT

Keep going back to the text. "If anyone wishes to come after Me, he must deny himself, and take up his cross daily and follow Me" (Luke 9:23; see also Matthew 16:24; Mark 8:34). Few Scriptures are known better or quoted more often than this one. Does it say what we make it say? Few Scriptures are more misunderstood and misused than this one. What does it mean to take up my cross daily?

(1) *Exclusive*. This could be one of the most harsh statements Jesus made. The statement is dogmatic, intolerant, rigid, basic, terse, mandatory, and eternally vital. Jesus said you are either "in" or "out." He gave no "ifs, ands, or buts." He said, "Whoever does not carry his own cross and come after Me cannot be My disciple" (Luke 14:27); "So then, none of you can be My disciple who does not give up all his own possessions" (Luke 14:33). The cross calls for death. We must die to self, sin, and society. Crosses are costly. Basically, we have only three problems: "me, myself, and I." We must die to all three! Superficial views of the cross make weak Christians. We cannot compromise the cross. The Christian life is not always easy and happy. Will we pay the price? You die to yourself when you give up your rights to yourself. Jesus is Lord. The only qualification that you need to become a Christian is to admit being a lost sinner. No one but sinners can apply.

We know we need to believe in God. We also need to know that God believes in us. The power to live the Epistles is found in the cross. We are pardoned—not paroled. We do not live like convicts. Only men who have been saved from sin can bring others to Christ. We must never forget that God lives only in "earthen vessels" (2 Corinthians 4:7; see Acts 9:15, 16). Christians must become vessels of honor (2 Timothy 2:20, 21). All of us must develop our own relationship with God. We cannot afford to live in doubt and visit our faith. We must live in faith and abandon our doubt.

(2) *Daily.* "Ouch, this hurts!" Daily? Christianity is a life—not a moment. Paul tersely said, ". . . I die daily" (1 Corinthians 15:31). Life is daily—so is Christianity. We need daily bread (Matthew 6:11) and daily spiritual bread (Acts 17:11; Hebrews 3:13). The early church had daily additions (Acts 2:47; 16:5). We do not die once and stay dead. Daily death is a daily choice. Christians living crucified with Christ . . .

> . . . are facing only one direction.
> . . . can never turn back.
> . . . no longer have plans of their own.
> . . . have minds through which Christ thinks.
> . . . have hearts through which Christ loves.
> . . . have a voice through which Christ speaks.
> . . . have bodies through which Christ serves.

Carry your cross until you find someone who needs it more than you do—then give it to him. (You never will.)

(3) *My cross is not one of my many burdens.* Too many think, "This burden must be my cross to bear." Jesus said "cross," not "crosses." A cross is something we "take up," not something we "put up with." That thinking reduces Christians to victims. Galatians 2:20, 21 can be the most "self-filled" text in the Scriptures; it can also be the most

"self-surrendered" text. Eight personal pronouns are used in the passage. "I" appears five times; "me" appears three. What is the great paradox? Self-crucifixion allows true life. One can neither kill nor hurt a dead man. Some of us are not totally dead. The man who has died to everything has the ability to give up anything. Preachers, elders, deacons, and teachers have to die before they serve. The alabaster box has to be broken (see Mark 14:3).

(4) *My cross is not misery or sadistic martyrdom.* My cross represents joy, not pessimistic "doom and gloom" (see John 15:11–14; Romans 14:17; 15:13; Hebrews 12:2; James 1:2; 1 John 1:4; 3 John 4). Tragically, we have preached guilt without grace; we must know grace before we preach guilt. Do not preach self-sacrifice without joy. Do not reduce the gospel to stoicism. Taking up the cross is positive, not negative; it is joyous, not miserable. It results in victorious living, not neurotic martyrdom. We are called to live as the "forgiveness of God."

(5) *A sinner, in order to receive salvation, must die to himself and take up his cross daily.* These are two separate actions, not one. Do not confuse "self-denial" with "cross-bearing." What, then, is cross-bearing? It is forgiveness. We need fresh forgiveness daily. Yesterday's forgiveness is not for today or tomorrow. To take up my cross is to live forgiven and to forgive others every day. We cannot receive what we refuse to give. Until one accepts grace, he cannot learn mercy. The cross is our call to forgive. Each of us must write a book on the cross. I have written mine; now write yours!

The cross . . .
there is no other way!

QUESTIONS FOR STUDY AND DISCUSSION

1. Have sermons and hymns about the blood of Christ been included in recent worship services where you worship? Why is this important?
2. Give a brief summary of Leviticus. Why is the study of this book often neglected?
3. Contrast the system of sacrifices in the Old Testament with the New Testament plan of salvation. (Refer to Hebrews 9; 10.)
4. Illustrate Jesus' specific emphasis on His blood in comparison to the cross and His death.
5. What are some New Testament concepts connected with the blood of Jesus?
6. What does it mean to take up your cross daily?

THE CROSS AND MY SALVATION

A STUDY GUIDE

IAN TERRY

In reading this book, our hearts have been touched by the inestimable love that God and Jesus have for all humanity. We have been impressed by the awfulness of the universal sin of mankind that would require such a costly and painful sacrifice. Surely, we desire to have a harmonious relationship with God, who loves us so much and wants to lavish His blessings upon us for all eternity.

How, then, can we apprehend the salvation and forgiveness that Jesus made available through the cross? How can we receive the eternal life that Jesus agonized to provide?

Consider the following questions, and God will give you the answers through His Word as you read the associated Scriptures. We pray that you will make the appropriate response at the close of the study.

1. Why do we need the forgiveness that Jesus died to provide? (Romans 3:9–18, 23)
   Does this include you?

2. What must we do first to receive the forgiveness and eternal life that Jesus came to give? (John 3:16, 17; 8:24)
   Who must we believe that Jesus is? (Matthew 1:18–25)
   Why is it so important to believe in Jesus? (John 14:6; Acts 4:12)
   What must we believe that Jesus did to make it possible for us to be forgiven? (Matthew 20:28; Romans 5:8, 9)
   Do you believe in Jesus?

3. What is the next element in our response to Jesus? (Acts 17:30; 26:20)

What is repentance, and why is it essential? (Acts 3:19; Luke 13:3)

What considerations motivate us to repent? (Romans 2:4; 2 Thessalonians 1:7-9; 1 Peter 1:18, 19)

Are you going to turn your back on the sin that crucified Jesus and follow Him?

4. What is the third step in accepting Jesus' forgiveness? (Romans 10:9, 10)

Why is it so important to acknowledge Jesus and give your allegiance to Him? (Matthew 10:32, 33; 1 Timothy 6:12, 13)

Are you ready to confess your faith in Christ?

5. What is the final act of faith and obedience, at which point our sins are forgiven and we are saved? (Mark 16:16; Acts 2:38)

How does the Bible express the purpose of baptism? (Acts 22:16)

Is Bible baptism sprinkling, pouring, or immersion? (Acts 8:35–39; Romans 6:3, 4)

How does baptism relate to the saving act of Jesus—His death, burial, and resurrection? (Romans 6:3–11)

YOUR RESPONSE

Now that God, through His Word, has shown you how He wants you to respond to Jesus in receiving salvation and the forgiveness of your sins, are you ready to turn your back on sin and follow Him?

Are you ready to acknowledge Him as Lord and be buried and raised with Him through baptism, in the likeness of His saving act, for the forgiveness of your sins?

If you are ready to take this step of faith, contact the nearest church of Christ, and someone will assist you. If you are not sure where the nearest church is located, go to *churchzip.com* and type your location.